RIGHTEOUS POWER

IN A CORRUPT WORLD

—THE APPLICATION OF GOD'S LEADERSHIP STRATEGY —

by

Morris E. Ruddick

XULON
PRESS

ALSO AVAILABLE
BY MORRIS RUDDICK

THE JOSEPH-DANIEL CALLING: Facilitating the Release of the Wealth of the Wicked

GOD'S ECONOMY, ISRAEL AND THE NATIONS: Discovering God's Ancient Kingdom Principles of Business and Wealth

THE HEART OF A KING: The Leadership Measure of the Joseph-Daniel Calling

SOMETHING MORE: A Devotional Dimension for the Joseph-Daniel Calling

TABLE OF CONTENTS

SECTION III: MATURITY AS A BODY

SECTION IV: LEADERSHIP FOR CHANGE

APPENDIX

DEDICATION

My life has singularly been enriched with the quality of the relationships the Lord has brought my way. It has been key roles at significant times that have made the differences that have made a difference in what impact I've been able to contribute to the Kingdom. Because of that, the dedication selection for this and my previous four books has been a daunting experience.

Yet, because of the focus of this book, it is first and foremost dedicated to those we have been so honored to serve: those persecuted for their faith.

With that, is the mention of those friends who have served as gatekeepers, entrusting us with cherished relationships that opened the doors into the inner circles of those segments of the Body who pay such a high cost for their faith.

I also want to mention our many friends, Jewish brethren, who have taken the time to impart to us the richness of the Jewish roots to our faith.

Then, for our esteemed board and those serving as advisors, along with each one who has been led to contribute to making these "application" efforts possible.

In keeping with the focus of this book in applying the "God-centered, entrepreneurial community" model is the vital mentoring task played by my dear friend Dr. Bill Bolton, world-class expert on entrepreneurship, professor, author, business owner and committed Christian. I am similarly very grateful to Barry Harper, one of the two original founders of the organization that became Opportunity

International, for his great insights into the dynamics of mobilizing entrepreneurs in economically-challenged lands.

Finally and not least is the timely role and true example of Kingdom partnership with Pastors Michael and Brenda Walker, senior pastors of the one-new-man congregation of Church in the City-Beth Abraham of Denver. Their insatiable hungering for that something more in their congregational leadership and function as opportunity enablers for the broader community is a model for our time.

ACKNOWLEDGEMENTS

For their insightful and valued review of this manuscript, together with the impartation of a wisdom in keeping with the strategic nature of this effort, I want to express my deepest appreciation to Judy Haynes, Barbara Fox and David Works. I'm likewise most grateful to Mark Taylor for facilitating the Forward of this book from Bishop Bill Hamon.

I also am deeply indebted to those faithful and dear friends who have stood in the gap and upheld us with their prayers, as we have reached for more than what we could do in the natural. My gratefulness for the sacrifice and significant value of these sustaining prayers far exceeds what words might try to express.

Over the years, I've observed just how many of those I've become closest to have been ones far more talented than myself. My wife Carol is no exception. With that caveat, I want to acknowledge Carol's most capable and dedicated role and patience in encouraging my zeal and efforts. It's clearly been beyond the call of duty.

FORWARD
AND COMMENDATION

BILL HAMON

Bishop of Christian International Ministries Network (CIMN), Christian International Apostolic Network (CIAN) and CI Global Network (CIGN); author of almost two dozen books; forerunner and apostle for today's prophetic and apostolic movements.

This book is timely for the day in which we live. Morris Ruddick has received the revelation and wisdom to enable God's people to manifest God's Kingdom.

Morris speaks from years of successfully applying the principles of the Kingdom around the world that enable Christians to demonstrate God's righteous power in corrupt settings. He emphasizes the success principles to release God's blessings revealed in Deuteronomy 28. It begins with hearing and obeying the voice of the Lord. Every successful endeavor in the Bible was based on a person hearing the directive voice of God and then properly following through.

Noah, for instance, heard the voice of God to leave his established profession and go into the shipbuilding business. Because Noah obeyed the voice of the Lord and built the ark, his business stayed afloat while everyone else and their businesses were liquidated.

The Kingdom of God is destined to be exalted above all other Kingdoms of this world. The emphasis for today is on the Kingdom of God being demonstrated in every nation.

We preachers in the pulpit are called to bring revelation and training for the saints to be ministers in the marketplace who will serve as Kingdom influencers in their sphere of influence, whether in business, government, education, the professions or the media.

This book has the answers for those leading the way with change for the turbulent times in which we live. Every saint who wants to prosper during challenging times of famine like Isaac did needs to read and put into practice the proven principles found within this book.

ENDORSEMENTS

KENT HUMPHREYS
Ambassador, Fellowship of Companies for Christ/Christ@Work,
Business Owner

Morris Ruddick has given us a great Kingdom perspective with a wealth of sound wisdom on how to apply biblical business principles in a practical step by step manner. The teaching on Entrepreneurship alone is worth the price of the book. His experience as a trainer of business leaders globally provides insights that will be extremely helpful for all of us.

JUDY HAYNES
Co- Founder of the Christian Coalition; Political Consultant,
Business Owner

While reading Righteous Power in a Corrupt World I realized that this book was meant to be in the hands of every ministry leader who understands and embraces the partnership of ministry and marketplace. These biblical principals will be used in a revolutionary way of financing the work of the Kingdom. This book is definitely that "something more" for those called by God to extend their reach beyond all human capability to achieve His purpose.

PEARL KUPE
Founding President,
Kingdom Chamber of Commerce in Afrika (KCCA),
Business Owner, Attorney

The words *"a mantle of righteous power"* resonated deeply in my spirit after reading this book. *"Righteousness"* is the key word for this season. That makes this book a must read, not only for those operating in the Apostolic and Prophetic marketplace grace, but for the Body of Christ in general; those called as the ekklessia, the "called-out ones" who are to have dominion, take control and make a difference!

STEVE SNOW
Retired President, Automated Call Processing Corporation,
Former Group Product Manager, The Clorox Company

This useful book traces entrepreneurial concepts to Biblical passages and provides a scripture-based outline for starting and growing businesses in communities of believers. It will be very helpful to Christians in the third-world. Good work!

BARRY HARPER
Co-Founder of Opportunity International
CPA, Consultant, Entrepreneur, Organizer of the Presidential
Prayer Breakfast

Great read! This book provides much insight into the deeper issues faced by those taking entrepreneurship to the most needy! I am encouraged that there are men like Morris Ruddick who continue to "carry the torch". My many international experiences have born out his comments concerning the church and its people. "Small" business has been a grass roots foundation in the growth of the Kingdom. Our country's foundation began with 95% of America being small business and the church playing an integral part of those communities. I pray Morris continues the difficult journey on which he has embarked.

PREFACE

During a recent mission to Eastern Europe we encountered the unexpected. In the midst of a turbulent spiritual climate, born of a mix of witchcraft and former communist controls, we found a group of believers led by a committed, core band of modern-day Josephs operating in a high-level of biblical community. Despite the static they received, their influence was making an impact not only at the community level, but into seats of power of their national government.

Their role in their society was as it has been ordained and should be since God has had a people: employing righteous power in a corrupt world.

The employment of righteous power is the mantle we carry, as a people of God. We're called to bring His heart and presence into a dark world, as we let His light shine. It's a community function. However, it involves risk and carries a cost.

Righteous power goes against the grain. It doesn't operate like worldly power. Jesus described it as being a pathway that is narrow and difficult. In following this course, He made it clear that many were called, but few were chosen. It's a mantle that involves an identity, a maturity, a power and a function of leadership, as a people.

Righteous power builds and brings increase; it wields influence, and is a catalyst for opportunity that brings blessing to those in its sphere. It demonstrates the reality of God to people in darkness, with practicalities by the way life is lived with God.

The Challenge

The challenge in stewarding righteous power and staying the course of its difficult, narrow path is in getting the calling right. However, to get the calling right requires the right mantle, model and mandate. That premise delineates a cultural identity that supersedes its worldly context. It is a foundation outlined in the Word of God that has been demonstrated over the millennia by a people, known as God's chosen, the Jews.

Getting it right, as a people, has been described by Paul in Ephesians 4 as an issue driven by maturity. The convergence of the identity operating in community releases righteous power that becomes the catalyst to a spiritual dimension that results in those known by His Name operating as the head and not the tail.

During the early 70s, my wife Carol and I were touched by revival. Like many, we had believed in God, but hungered for the relevance and reality of God to be manifested. We began seeing that manifestation, as the Spirit of the Lord was moving and you didn't want to miss being a part. That hunger evoked in us, reaching for a dimension of "something more" that only could come from God. We weren't disappointed.

Our priorities shifted and we found opportunity in a fast-track of walking by faith and not by sight. It was a time of great change. That change was taking place all around us; and resulted in adjustments in our lifestyles and decisions in our reach for the "something more." Coming from the military, I understood community, commitment and discipline. We began absorbing the Word of God and learning to discern this pathway of being led by the Spirit. Then came radical change

In mid-stream, we left the security of a career I was building in the military to prepare for ministry. We hooked up with a ministry filled with other active, hungry participants and lived on a combined weekly salary of $25. In less than a year's time, the clear leading of the Spirit had moved us from Virginia Beach to Monterey, California and then settled us in Tulsa at Oral Roberts University, where the mandate is "to train up young people to hear God's voice and then to GO where God's light is dim."

The Reach

Following this time of preparation, in my God's Economy book I've described the unique way the Lord led me past standard expressions of ministry and into the world of business. Yet, at the core of what had begun in response to the move of the Spirit in the early 70's was this hunger for a life filled with the demonstration of the reality of God operating in our midst.

There came cycles in our pathway; cycles in which the vibrancy of revival wasn't always in the forefront. Nevertheless, the hunger I had for His presence led me into a disciplined pursuit of His Word and of intercession; and with that the outworking of this matter we refer to as our calling. For one clearly called into ministry, this pathway into business was at this time largely uncharted waters.

In the years that followed, we encountered diverse expressions of faith in those we linked with for purpose and community. We were drawn to others with the same hunger and also those who shared this unique mantle in the marketplace. Still, there seemed to be the sense of something more for which I continued to reach.

Then, without really having the background, I responded in obedience to God's guidance and started a business. It grew to become far more successful than I would have dreamed with an eventual full time staff of 27.

In that success and my zeal, my focus had become what I was faithfully doing for God. However, that was a major chink in my armor, since the subtle difference the Lord was looking for was not what I was doing for Him, but rather what the Lord wanted to do through me.

At that juncture in the early 80s, there came an unexpected dip in the primary market our business served. While I say unexpected, the reality is that there had been a sense of looming change, had I been listening to the Lord more carefully to respond. However, success can have that type of impact and I missed the turn.

The result was a long, painful downturn of our business that eventually resulted in our shutting it down. After spiritually digging in more deeply, some invaluable corporate experience and then recovery, I emerged as an entrepreneur with a much more flexible format, which allowed the outworking of something very key the

Lord had spoken to me during this time of turmoil; that He had called me into an interlinking between secular business enterprises with overriding Kingdom objectives. Again, that story can be gleaned in my "God's Economy" book.

During this same time frame the aura of revival, that had been so significant in motivating me to drop a career path to follow the Lord, had gone through its own time of disruption. Between the extremes of theologues who shunned God's power outside their own frame of reference, and those whose illusions of grandeur over their accomplishments for God seduced them from the narrow path; the spontaneity of the revival had waned. The reality was that what had been a movement now lay entrusted in the hearts of a generation of individuals and smaller communities.

Significantly for me, this word about an "interlinking of business and ministry" was a bit out-of-the-box for the models I had seen. So the reach for this unique focus became more fervent and a key focus in my prayers and what I began seeking for my business activities.

In the time just prior to the Tianamen Square standoff, I found myself in Asia gripped with the realities of those persecuted for their faith. This significant encounter deeply stirred within me the prospects for how business might strategically serve those down-trodden for their faith. It also awakened the love I had had for a similar group of Asians I had served with during my Marine Corps days in the 60s, whose believers were also now living under severe persecution.

Paralleling these events, with the support of our local congregation, we began a unique home group designed to reach out to the international community in our city. Our approach seemed to break traditional molds with a respectful, prayer-filled party atmosphere to the gatherings. Not many weeks after we started this effort, the Lord brought in an unexpected dimension, as several members of our group were instantly healed. The attendance that followed multiplied with people who were hungry for the reality of God; and were receiving it.

The Turning

Then in the early to mid-90s, as one who might be described as a mature believer and a leader, two key things occurred. I became acquainted with an expression of the Body I had never seen before; Messianic Judaism. With that, came an awareness of the operation of community that went beyond any previous expressions of the Body in which I had taken part.

In that same time frame, two other significant developments emerged. With the flexibility of my business activities, I first began pursuing and assisting with mission relationships. The second was the birth of the SIGN (www.strategicintercession.org) ministry, which carried with it a mandate that required a diligent pursuit of God's heart.

All this became a paradigm shift for me. It challenged all the traditional models, not to speak of the focus of the mandate of my calling. Likewise, the time I spent with the Lord took on new dimensions, as I also began discerning truths in the Word I had never seen before. With this shift came a merging of it all.

It was at that point that I began to see what I describe as "collateral fruit" from my time in seeking God, which had taken on a proactive dimension of capturing in writing the insights I was gleaning during my times of prayer.

In 1997, I served as a part of the executive committee that launched an initiative in Israel to provide food, clothing and housewares to new immigrants through local Messianic Jewish congregations. This initiative began a shift in the perceptions of the local population for the pioneering, but extremely persecuted Israeli Jewish believers. Around the same time, I began taking on assignments with Israel's Office of the Chief Scientist's business incubator program.

In the late-90s, I was a part of an ICCC board, spearheaded by Dale Neill that produced a most unusual TV series for China's educational TV channel. Knowing that the roots to free-enterprise were biblical, this educational channel approached Mr. Neill on producing a series on "How to Start a Business." However, government protocol demanded something less than an overt expression of the Christian faith. The resolve agreed on was that the scripture used to explain biblical principles of business would be prefaced with "it is written." Following the first viewing of this series, a survey revealed the part of the show the audience liked the most was the segments on "it is written."

In that same time-frame, I was sent to Ethiopia to make an evaluation of business opportunity for a community of persecuted and impoverished Ethiopian Jewish believers. Their plight resulted in my crying out to the Lord in prayer for His answer to the bondage they lived under. That heart-cry converged with ones I had already been praying, for over a decade: for the brethren in Asia's persecuted church.

It was at that juncture, that the articles for SIGN began turning into books. With that came God's guidance to start applying the model, the mandate and mantle that I had been writing about.

This application of these principles became the birth of the God's economy entrepreneurial startup program that we began taking to lands of persecution. These efforts have served to develop scores of enterprises ranging from businesses large enough to feed a family to privately owned companies with numerous employees to community-run ventures. From the start, these simple efforts have brought results that could only have been attributed to God. Simultaneously, there was another dimension to these efforts of assisting the brethren (Acts 15:32), who against all odds were taking monumental risks involving extremely high costs in their reach for the something more.

Without planning it that way, I began realizing that the Lord had brought us full-circle. We were working with believers, whose simple faith in believing God's Word, coupled with a priority in seeing the reality of God manifest, were operating as carriers of revival with amazing things happening in their midst.

This book combines what has unfolded from a walk of faith that has fervently sought God's heart; with a strategy for change we have discovered in God's Word and in the Jewish roots to the faith that we have been applying in impossible situations with extraordinary results in lands persecuted for their faith.

Each of the main chapters represent modules from our God's economy business startup program that we have implemented in a range of nations that have included, but are not limited to Israel,

Belarus, Russia, Botswana, Nigeria, India and Vietnam.

The core of this message provides a practical outline for godly leadership and influence to impact your congregation, community and nation by nurturing a spiritual maturity that:

- Genuinely and confidently discerns His voice and counsel,
- Becomes adept at interacting with the Lord in applying His guidance, and
- Enters a path of cooperative oneness with Him that refines the implementation and timing of His purpose and agendas tied to your calling.

This application of truth represents a pathway that Jesus described as the Kingdom pathway that historically has been the way God has led the most unlikely people, in the most impossible situations to bring about the most remarkable results.

It is the application of righteous power in a corrupt world.

SECTION I:

IDENTITY AS A PEOPLE

CHAPTER 1

THE MANDATE, MODEL AND MANTLE

*"You will be called the repairer of the breach,
the restorer of paths to dwell in."*
Isaiah 58:12b

From the ghettoes over the centuries, the Jewish people have strategically influenced kings, merchants and power brokers; with their influence laying the foundations for the economic, moral, legal and governmental systems we now call Western civilization. Despite being only a quarter of one percent of the world's population the Jewish people have been awarded 23 percent of all Noble Prizes and 27 percent since the holocaust. Their impact has exceeded the best the world has had to offer.

In contrast to this remarkable impact and despite Nigeria's claim to being the most evangelized nation on the continent of Africa, at this writing, it remains one of the most lawless and impoverished. Likewise, notwithstanding the most valiant efforts of both the humanitarians and the Church, in 2007 Haiti had ten times the amount of aid as it did investment.

More than two-thirds of the world has little or no middle class. Some estimates are as high as three-fourths of the globe's population who live on less than $2 a day in conditions described by the Psalmist as oppression, affliction and sorrow. As God's people, we have the truth, but there is a need for its unfettered application to bring meaningful change.

The issue is transformation; the need for change that endures with the ripples of God's blessings that demonstrate the reality of God, that draws people to Himself. The gap between the societal impact of the Jewish people and the role of the Church suggests there being something more.

In early 1999, I was in Ethiopia to make an evaluation of business opportunity for a community of impoverished, persecuted believers. The obvious solution was cottage industries, but with more than 30 years experience as a business consultant at the time, I knew enduring change would require more than a contrived, Western model.

I began crying out to the Lord for answers. The answer that began unfolding from that heart-cry has developed into a program we have extended to the persecuted and oppressed around the world, with results that have exceeded our expectations. It is a program that takes God's most unlikely and makes them the head rather than the tail, in the most adverse of circumstances.

It is a program that had its start in peeling back the trappings of Western, twentieth century models and gleaning the wisdom that has endured since the time of Abraham.

God's Catalyst for Change

Throughout the Bible are stories of ones who have brought change to society under great adversity. We call them the heroes of faith.

The solution involves breaking the bondage of corruption and releasing that "something more" that brings lasting change. That something more operated under Joseph the Patriarch. He demonstrated it under some of the most adverse and improbable of circumstances. Daniel exercised it when immersed in a culture of sorcery. David, as a most unlikely candidate, prevailed with it and ushered his people into a time of great unity and peace.

God's catalyst for change builds and brings increase. It wields influence and creates opportunity. It releases blessing to those within the sphere of its operation.

Over the ages, God's footprint has been marked by ordinary

people doing extraordinary things. It is the simple things that confound the wise. It all pivots on hearing the voice of the Lord and obeying. Like Joseph during his tenure as an Egyptian slave, the results will defy the odds for those willing to pay the cost.

The Mandate and the Model

The mandate and the model are the foundation. The world is searching for a people who will demonstrate the reality of God operating in their midst. Establishing God's Kingdom authority goes beyond ethics, obeying His Word and being nice people. It goes beyond interim stratagems fueled by pop-Christian culture. It typically runs in the face of what is embraced as the status quo.

"These who have turned the world upside down have come here too!" Acts 17:6

The original mandate was described at creation: "Let us make man in our image and let them have dominion [over all the earth]." God made man to rule over the work of His hands. It is the mandate of His people for dominion.

The model was established by Abraham. Abraham operated a God-centered, entrepreneurial community. Moses outlined the primary principles of the model in the book of Deuteronomy.

The Mantle of Abraham

The previous examples of the heroes of faith conform to a dimension that has operated historically in the Jewish people.

Their impact on society over the ages reflects "something more" that cannot be explained by natural abilities. Even within this generation, a disproportionate ratio of technology solutions has come from Israel since the nineties. From cell phone technologies, to PC operating systems, to voice mail, to ingestible micro-video cameras, to computerized administration of medications, Israel's global impact defies any normal expectation of results.

This dynamic began when the Lord spoke to Abram and said: "Get out of your country, from your father's house to a land I will show you. I will make you a great nation and I will bless you. I will make your name great and you shall be a blessing. I will bless those who bless you and I will curse those who curse you; and through you all the families of the earth will be blessed." Gen 12:2-3

The something more is the mantle of Abraham "to be blessed to be a blessing."

The mandate and model combine to demonstrate the reality of God through which the mantle of Abraham, to be blessed to be a blessing, has served as a light to the nations. The issue for results is the supernatural, the outgrowth of working in oneness with God. More than just faith in God, it's cooperation with God for His purposes of repairing the breach and restoring the paths to dwell in.

The Dynamic

The distinctive is our identity in God and the stewardship of the mantle of the "something more" the world lacks.

"Creation itself longs for the revealing of the sons of God; that it might be delivered from the bondage of corruption, as it gains entrance into this glorious freedom." Romans 8:21

The Lord gives gifts to men to bring increase and blessing. The gifts combine to interact with the mix of the economic, community and spiritual dimensions of His Word to reset the status quo.

George Washington Carver was a man born into slavery in the early 1860s in the US. When the slaves were freed, George Washington Carver went on to develop a gift he had in botany. Then, during his early 30s, as a committed believer, he prayed the most audacious prayer. He asked the Lord to show him the secrets of the universe! The Lord answered George Washington Carver and said, "Little man, the secrets of the universe would destroy you; but I'll show you the secrets of the peanut."

During the next ten years, George Washington Carver developed 325 inventions involving the peanut. He created an industry that wasn't there before and in the process, this man who had been born into slavery changed the course of his nation.

The gifts combine to break the mold and operate against the odds when we adhere to the voice of the Lord and obey.

The Process

Scripture tells us there are a variety of gifts designed for the common good.

Our economic community development program that operates against the odds of persecution and adversity gives focus to a mix of gifts that begin in individual believers. The natural gifts are based on each person being able to do something better than most other people, when developed. The spiritual gifts begin with the Romans 12 motivational gifts, which determine how individual believers flow most naturally in the Spirit. The Romans 12 gifts include leader, mercy, serving, giving, exhorter, teacher and prophetic. . The entrepreneurial gift is a reflection of God's nature to create, innovate, build and multiply. When these basic gifts in an individual are in right alignment, they release a gift of the exponential, which is a multiplied factor that goes beyond normal standards of increase.

The gifts are stirred and released through the anointing and become the foundation for what we call one's destiny or calling. The sowing of the gifts yields enlargement. The impact of the gifts multiplies when applied with the community dynamic of tz'dakah or "righteous charity."

Beginning with the model and the mandate, our program employs a sequence of modules to activate the mantle of Abraham through purposeful development of entrepreneurial community. The primary modules include: Defining and Releasing the Gifts; Hearing God on Business Decisions; The Pathway of Holy Spirit-Directed Planning; God's Economy, Entrepreneurship and Success; Stewardship; Community-Building; Enabling Opportunity; and Building Community Builders.

Defining and Releasing the Gifts. The "gifts" bear on one's calling. They begin at the individual level as the mix of natural, spiritual and entrepreneurial gifts mature and begin releasing the exponential. Change begins taking root when the diversity of individual contributions melds and begins operating at the community level.

Hearing God on Business Decisions. Hearing God on specific decisions begins with an interactive partnership with Him at the individual level. Within community, the effectiveness of employing the model is facilitated through servant-leadership that advances agendas toward the common good.

The Pathway of Holy Spirit Directed Planning. Planning is a pathway of purpose employing the combined gifts that is guided by the Spirit. Community-wise it is the building process with the Lord as the cornerstone and those anointed as leaders paving the way by which each one plays their part, based on their individual gifts.

God's Economy, Entrepreneurship and Success. Free enterprise in its purist sense is outlined in Deuteronomy, and further developed in Psalms, Proverbs, the Prophets, the parables of Jesus and teachings of Paul. God's economy is key to the model and mandate. Spotting opportunity and purposefully knowing what to do is the basis of Kingdom entrepreneurship. True success is based on the type of increase that assumes the responsibility and pays the cost to build community.

Stewardship. Over half the scriptures on righteousness are in the context of stewardship. Making God your Senior Partner, in practice, will bring increase and dominion. When the mandate is aligned with the model and applied in the right way, it will serve to overcome the bondage of corruption.

Community Building. Building community requires the convergence of fundamental mind-sets: Kingdom, Hebraic, entrepreneurial and tz'dakah/charity. God gave community itself as a gift and means of protection, to nurture opportunity and to wield the power and influence in standing against darkness.

Enabling Opportunity. Leadership employing the model and mandate within both top-down and bottom-up community enterprises, will manifest in opportunity that provides solutions in the face of overwhelming odds of adversity.

Building Community Builders. Enabling opportunity is a process of mentoring new entrepreneurial stewards whose mind-sets and mix of gifts are directed toward building community.

Each of these dimension combine to provide the framework for the way the Kingdom is designed to operate. Jesus' earthly ministry laid out the strategy for actuating the Kingdom dynamic on the earth. Planning with the Holy Spirit unlocks opportunity that serves to create, innovate, build and bring increase and blessing. Jesus said that we are to be a community set on a hill that cannot be hidden (Matt 5:14).

The Pathway

For far too many in the Church, the Kingdom is limited to the hereafter and the millennium. Jesus came to reconnect God's chosen to Himself and restore the foundations as it was in the beginning, with the model operated by Abraham. He outlined a pathway He described as narrow and difficult, but one that imparts Life.

With that Jesus laid an axe to the root of blindness created by the unholy alliances between the religious elite and the power brokers of the world. He outlined the foundations for true leadership that would destroy the works of the devil and the bondage of corruption; and release God's Kingdom rule.

Entering God's Kingdom and bearing fruit is what differentiates leaders from followers; the called and the chosen (Matt 20:16).

Jesus' parables unfold the dynamics of the Kingdom of God; the priorities, the issues, how it works and the mantle of Abraham. "The first shall be last and the last first" parable and the parable of the two sons working within the vineyard of the Kingdom address position and faithfulness. The parable of the talents deals with the issue of stewardship; then the sheep and the goats bears on those who truly assume the mantle as the King says: "Come you blessed of my Father, enter...."

Many Kingdom keys seem as contradictions to the way the world operates and views success: We advance by yielding. Honor comes through humility. Wisdom is found in simplicity. Making your assets multiply will bring promotion. Growth comes by giving to others. We extend love to our enemies. Our purpose in life comes through giving it up. We receive when giving. Perfect love eliminates fear. In our weakness we are made strong. Ownership increases by sharing. We bless those who curse us. We lead by serving.

In short, we are not called to be or operate like everyone else. We are called to be in the world, but not of the world. We're called to make a difference that transforms.

The Domain for Change

God-centered entrepreneurial community is both the model and the catalyst. Community was designed as a safe place with God at the center and His people sharing a common purpose as they apply the combined diversity of their gifts. It is the group-setting through which God's Kingdom rule operates. It is a light shining in the darkness, because God is there.

God-centered entrepreneurial community is God's people operating beyond that place of human effort turning the ordinary into the extraordinary. It is an entrepreneurial assembly of God's own operating in supernatural increase to make a difference by enabling others. With it comes the multiplied impact of the combined potential from within the group, as it flows in oneness with Him.

Dominion comes from a process of stewarding the gifts to establish God's Kingdom rule and authority in a given sphere. Dominion involves daily cooperation with God, by applying His Truth and heeding His voice. Coming together in community, on the Kingdom pathway, wields the power to reverse the curse.

The original "dominion" mandate and Jesus' Matthew 28 mandate conform to where the gospel of salvation and the social gospel collide with the gospel of the Kingdom. The Gospel of the Kingdom is the gospel people run to because they see the reality and demonstration of God operating in their midst as described in Acts 5: "Great fear came upon all the Church and upon ALL who heard of these things."

It bears on when the exponential gift is actuated within community, as it fulfills the mandate given to Abraham, to be blessed to be a blessing. The impact is prophesied in Isaiah 58 as a people who, against all odds, have been equipped to fix anything; "to repair the breach and restore the paths;" whose complete mantle is described by Paul in Romans 11 as bringing life from the dead.

In challenging times, knowing what to do takes something more than the best the world has to offer. The original mandate and the model, together with the strategy of the Kingdom, operating with the mantle of Abraham; provide the seedbed from which the Kingdom grows, repairs the breach and restores the paths to dwell in.

"In all matters of wisdom and understanding about which the king examined them, he found them ten times better than all the magicians and astrologers who were in all his realm." Daniel 1:20

CHAPTER 2

THE GIFTS,
ANOINTING AND CALLING

"Now the LORD spoke to Moses, saying:
'See, I have called by name, Bezalel. I have filled him
with the Spirit of God in wisdom, in understanding, in knowledge,
and in all kinds of craftsmanship.'"
Exodus 31:1-3

There are a variety of gifts designed for the common good. When the calling is in harmony with God's purpose and in cooperation with the anointing, an added dimension tied to the gifts begins to unfold.

In applying our business startup program in lands of persecution, identifying an individual's "mix of gifts" represents the starting point in the process to overcome the adversities in establishing a successful, Spirit-led business.

This mix of gifts begins with what we refer to as the natural gift. The natural gift represents something that a person can do better than most other people, when the gift has been developed. Next are the spiritual gifts. The spiritual gifts are the Romans 12 motivational gifts (teacher, exhorter, leader, giver, prophetic, mercy, server), which describe how an individual believer flows most naturally in the Spirit.

Then there is a dimension of God's nature to create, innovate, build and multiply, that operates in varying degrees in every believer.

We refer to this dynamic as the entrepreneurial gift. Not to be confused with a natural gift of being an entrepreneur, this entrepreneurial/ "creative, innovative, building" gift enhances the natural and spiritual gifts operating under the anointing, and paves new ground.

So, when these three basic elements of gifts in an individual are in right alignment, they release the exponential, which is a multiplying factor that produces results beyond normal standards of increase.

In short, the gifts are stirred and released through the anointing and become the foundation for what we call one's destiny or calling. The sowing of the gifts will yield enlargement. The impact of the gifts multiplies when applied with the community dynamic of tz'dakah or "righteous charity." The long-term benefit of the gifts rightly applied extends ripples of blessings to both the one bestowing and the recipients.

"Do you see a man skilled in his work? He will stand before kings; he will not stand before obscure men." Proverbs 22:29

The Dynamic of the Gifts

Many years ago, when I was in my early 30s, I was preparing myself for the calling I knew God had on my life. I had spent a year at a Christian university immersed in God's Word and in an environment designed to prepare young people to be a light where God's light was dim. I then responded to a distinct leading of the Spirit to extend my time of preparation at a secular university.

However, I found myself in over my head with some of the required courses in statistics. These classes included candidates for both Masters and Doctorate degrees. I studied, prepared weekly assignments and even sought special help, but still simply didn't grasp what was being presented. Despite what seemed as an impossible, uphill journey, I prayed for understanding. At one point, I came across a scripture in Psalm 119 that said: "I'll make you wiser than your teachers." While the potential of that word riveted me, at the time my grasp of the subject simply did not seem to be taking hold. On the night before the mid-term exam, I wept before the Lord because I felt I was going to fail and be a bad witness for the Lord.

So, despite pulling out every stop to prepare, not to speak of my despondent heart cry to the Lord the night before, I didn't feel any better as I walked into the room to take the exam. I put my name on the exam and read the first question. It almost startled me, because upon reading that question, I seemed to have a full understanding of everything the question posed. I read the second question: same thing. It wasn't an issue of knowing the answers: I had *the understanding* on what was being asked. I went through all the questions that way. While I wasn't fully sure what had just taken place, it was with a sense of elation that I handed in the exam.

I wasn't the first one to complete it, however. Three other grad students were in the hall complaining. The doctoral candidate who always seemed to have the answers in class was saying: "This professor is sadistic; that's the hardest test I've ever had in this subject." My elation took a dive and I began questioning what I had thought had happened to me as I had taken the exam.

A week later, the professor came into class with a handful of papers and a grim look on his face. It was our graded exams. After inferring that we were a substandard group of grape-sucking hedonists, he noted that the median grade was a 62. Then he started handing out the exams by calling the name of each student along with announcing their grade. One of the doctoral candidates had a 29 (out of 100). The star student had a 72. By the time he got to my name, I had braced myself; with little expectation for a passing grade. But after calling my name, he looked up and then back at my exam; and then announced my name again with a grade of 98.

God gave me a gift; not of a grade on the exam, but in my understanding of statistics. The word of *"I'll make you wiser than your teachers"* proved to be true, as I had to go to a professor in advanced statistics for what I wound up executing for my final thesis. This "gift" became a foundation for researching and evaluating decisions in business settings and gave me entrance into the consulting business. It eventually became the foundation for my starting and operating my own consulting business, as well as sharing co-authorship on three business texts.

What took place in that exam illustrates several key spiritual dynamics needed to enter the dimension of God's economy. The most pivotal of these dynamics is hearing and cooperating with the Holy Spirit. This is where the gifts are enhanced and become uniquely linked to the anointing and calling. I'm going to address the topic of hearing God, of applying the gifts in cooperation with the Holy Spirit for a higher purpose in the next chapter.

What took place in that exam also reflects the Kingdom dynamic of God's strength being manifested in our weaknesses. Still another of the dynamics bears on how the mix, or combination of gifts operate within an individual. It also illustrates how the factor of authority operates when combined with the anointing and calling to bring change; even more so when the diversity of gifts is applied within the context of community. Not to be considered least in these dynamics is the role of prevailing.

However, let's begin by addressing how the gifts, anointing and calling are linked.

Linking the Gifts, the Anointing and the Calling

The "gifts" are foundational to one's calling. They begin at the individual level. As the gifts are applied and mature, change begins taking root as the diversity of individual contributions melds into becoming impactful at the community level.

One's combined gifts are developed and refined through service to others. As they are yielded to God and His purpose, then the anointing for the combined gifts is released and nurtured. The calling evolves from the individual's mix of gifts and the anointing operating together over time. The process brings maturity to the gifts, as an individual yields himself to the Holy Spirit, refines the anointed gifts, and uses them for service in purposeful cooperation with the Lord.

Once again, the operating model was established by Abraham: the God-centered, entrepreneurial community. The entrepreneurial involves pioneers taking risks; breaking the mold and bringing increase and blessing for the common good. The purpose for the operation of the gifts then will always benefit and build community. The God-centered dimension means the Lord is actively involved as an integral part of the process, not just passively acknowledged or sought as an afterthought.

The Anointing, Calling and Gifts Working Together

So the combined gifts are developed to serve others. Proper alignment and development of the natural, spiritual and entrepreneurial will bring an exponential level of increase. As the gifts are prayerfully developed and enhanced, revelation and the anointing for the gifts will follow. The momentum that evolves from the gifts and the anointing operating together will define and release the calling. This divine interaction, faithfully applied, brings maturity to the process, as the added dimension of God's higher purposes is unveiled.

The example I gave of my graduate school exam reflected a "natural gift." It was only the beginning in a life-long process that began working together with my spiritual gifts to shape my calling.

My primary (Romans 12) spiritual gifts have always been that of a leader-teacher, with a secondary prophetic (intercession) gift. The focus of the gift given to me in that exam proved to be foundational to becoming a consultant (leader-teacher) and entrepreneur whose mix of prophetic insights and analytical/research-driven approach paved the way for unique problem-solving results. However, after twenty some-odd years in this consulting role, the foundation of my mix of gifts began to shift into serving another arena. That catalyst was the operation of the entrepreneurial.

The entrepreneurial gift is what gives rise to paving new ground. Again, the entrepreneurial is drawn from God's nature within us to "create, innovate, build and multiply." Some believers have the entrepreneurial as their primary natural gift (a special ability to spot opportunity and turn it into a business enterprise), but more often than not, the entrepreneurial is an enhancement of our combined natural and spiritual gifts operating under the anointing.

The birth of the SIGN ministry (www.strategicintercession.org) that targeted first understanding God's heart; and from that what we refer to as the Issachar context (understanding the times and knowing what to do) began releasing an entirely new dimension into my life-purpose and calling. While I have had secular consulting clients in the past who have commented that the Conclusions/Recommendations to my assignments have been prophetic; the two-plus decades of experience of working with senior decision-makers in multinational and Fortune 500 companies cultivated not only a planning mind-set, but a scrutiny and excellence that now was being applied to embracing God's heart in an effort to discern the tempo of the times with the intention of gleaning insights into strategically responding spiritually as a Body.

From this foundation in the mid-90s came a focus and a perspective from the posts I sent out from SIGN. Parenthetically, it should be noted that one of the charges the Lord gave me in developing these posts was that I was NOT to be reading or listening to what any other spiritual leaders were saying on these topics. My primary source of input for the first four years of the SIGN ministry was the Word of God and my prayer closet. From that came my first marketplace books. Then from those books was birthed the God's economy entrepreneurial program that we have taken around the world, but with a focus given to lands of persecution and corruption.

Prevailing with the Gifts

While the example of my grad school mid-term clearly illustrates the importance of reaching for and in paying the cost of prevailing for the individual gift; the example of a career as a market planning consultant that has transitioned into a unique global niche ministry punctuates the importance of continuing to seek the Lord (and His anointing) in allowing your calling and destiny to mature and unfold.

Prevailing with the gifts cannot be based on presumption or the forcing of issues. The process takes time. It MUST be a faith-response to not just hearing from God, but the ongoing alignment with God in the process. When that takes place, prevailing with the gifts advances the believer to the place of God's intervention that provides the supernatural means of opening otherwise impossible gateways.

Even then, when the supernatural is released, it is not an end to itself, but a means to set the stage for the next level of intervention, as the journey with God unfolds. My graduate school miracle, as remarkable as it was; was the passage into a dimension of my calling that would not have otherwise taken place.

God's Authority to Bring Change

When the gifts, the anointing and one's purposeful calling in

God are aligned, they release God's authority to bring change. The bottom line is that anointing the combined gifts will nurture and enhance the calling.

"A man's gift makes room for him and brings him before great men."
Proverbs 18:16

When rightly aligned within community, the administration of the diversity of gifts will actuate the change that builds community. When Joseph the Patriarch was Potiphar's slave, Potiphar recognized the blessing of God that came from Joseph's stewardship (Gen 39:2-5). Once he realized the authority of God operating through Joseph, Potiphar gave Joseph his authority and put Joseph over his entire household.

Yet, applying righteous power in corrupt settings can carry a cost. In Joseph's case, this process was unrighteously circumvented through spiritual backlash, resulting in his imprisonment. Yet, due to the stewardship of his gifts, the same thing happened. When the jailer discerned God's authority operating in Joseph, he entrusted his authority to Joseph and put him in charge of the other prisoners (Genesis 39:21-23).

So it was that when Joseph was brought before Pharaoh because of his reputation to interpret dreams, Pharaoh discerned the spiritual reality of God's authority operating through Joseph.

"So Pharaoh said to his servants: 'Can we find such a one as this, a man in whom is the Spirit of God?' Then Pharaoh said to Joseph, 'Inasmuch as God has shown you all this, there is no one as discerning and wise as you. You shall be over my house, and all my people shall be ruled according to your word...'" Genesis 41:39-41

Joseph's natural gift of leadership, his spiritual gift of the prophetic and the entrepreneurial that paves new ground that had operated under the most adverse of circumstances in Potiphar's house and then prison, had matured to the level that Joseph knew what to do when posed with the challenges facing Pharaoh.

Joseph's destiny unfolded in the face of impossible obstacles, through his selfless, faithful sowing of righteous power through his anointed gifts. The process became the catalyst for change and the release of God's blessings and purposes for Joseph, for Egypt and for God's chosen people.

"He who speaks from himself seeks his own glory; but He who seeks the glory of the One who sent Him is true, and no unrighteousness is in Him." John 7:18-19

In the next two chapters we will address the issue of planning in cooperation with the Holy Spirit. This proactive interaction with the Lord can then serve as the means to develop and enhance the combined gifts; launch and operate a purposeful business; or proactively mentor a group of believers.

CHAPTER 3

HOLY SPIRIT PLANNING

"The sons of Issachar, who had understanding of the times,
to know what Israel ought to do."
1 Chronicles 12:32 NKJV

After David was made King uniting Israel, the various communities came together, each serving their unique function that benefited the common good. The sons of Issachar operated as the planners. They understood the times and knew what to do.

Planning is the systematic employment of wisdom to map out the best steps, or strategies, to maximize the benefit of the process for the one(s) involved and the end-result for the broader community.

A planning mind-set sets leaders apart from followers. In Exodus 18:20 Moses' father-in-law outlined the basic tenets for the dynamic in which leaders nurture and build a community; with a foundation of the principles and precepts; followed by outlining the path in which they must walk; before giving them the work that they must do.

Good planning maps out the pathway. It is a mark of good stewardship. Planning engenders the discipline and maturity needed within community. When employed in conjunction with wise stewardship, planning is the means by which we fulfill the mandate, to rule over the work of His hands.

Anointed Planning
Anointed planning means the Holy Spirit is uniquely involved.

Proactive Holy Spirit planning has been a distinguishing characteristic of those we refer to as the heroes of faith. It incorporates an ongoing big-picture response that embraces the model; of being God-centered, entrepreneurial and community-focused. It is the means to the end of employing righteous power within a community-building setting.

In this context, the Lord serves a central, interactive role in the planning process. Anointed planning pivots on faith-responses to God's guidance. As outlined in Proverbs 3:5,6 this pivots on trusting the Lord for His input. God has always had a plan and a purpose for His own; individually and as a people. From the days of Noah, those whose accomplishments have become examples for the generations have been those who have sought and aligned themselves with that plan and purpose. Again, that plan and purpose has its foundation based on the biblical model, mandate and mantle outlined in Chapter 1.

So it is that learning to discern God's direction and wisdom for our individual lives, for a congregation, for a business or for a community is developed through the proactive process of seeking Him.

Genesis 26 outlines a story about Isaac that took place in a most challenging set of circumstances. In the first few verses of this chapter we learn that there was famine in the land. Nothing was growing. Isaac was in preparation to go to Egypt and the Lord intervened and told him:

"Dwell in this land, and I will be with you and bless you; for to you and your descendants I give all these lands, and I will perform the oath which I swore to Abraham your father." Genesis 26:3-4

A few verses further, we learn that Isaac obeyed God and sowed despite the famine:

"Then Isaac sowed in that land, and reaped in the same year a hundredfold; and the Lord blessed him. So the man began to prosper, and continued prospering until he became very prosperous; for he had possessions of flocks and possessions of herds and a great number of servants." Genesis 26:12-14

Gleaning God's Guidance

The principle to be gleaned from this is that when you hear the voice of the Lord and obey, the outcome will be much more than what might be accomplished in the natural. From the time that God has had a people, extraordinary things have been accomplished by those who have sought to hear His voice and then were obedient.

Eric Morey is an Israeli believer and friend of mine. Eric is the founder of the unique retail site on the waterfront of the Galilee known as the Galilee Experience. The Galilee Experience grew to become a favorite site for both Israeli and international tourists visiting that region of Israel. At a time when this business was doing well and profits stable, the Lord spoke to Eric to expand his operation into a catalog business.

Eric hesitated, since it would require significant investment and additional staff to manage this new dimension to an already very busy, growing business. Yet, Eric knew the voice of the Lord and complied. Then, several months after the catalog business was launched, the second Intifada hit Israel. This Intifada had a severe impact on Israeli tourism. For some in the tourism business, revenues were down as much as 95 percent. Sadly, many tourism-focused businesses closed their doors.

However for Eric, as the tourists visiting the Galilee Experience declined, his new catalog business of Israeli-products increased. During this extended down-time for tourism, the catalog business kept the Galilee Experience open.

Getting Specific in Hearing God

The assumptions for hearing God with specific decisions while planning are three-fold. First, is that you are born-again spiritually and called by God. Next is that you have something to offer in serving others with the focus of your planning. That may be in developing your gifts, planning for a business, guiding a congregation or the planning to bring change to a community or society. The final assumption is simply that you know how to plan and organize. These basic assumptions are all that is required to launch into a purposeful planning interaction with the Holy Spirit.

The first level in discerning God's guidance is through ethics and righteousness. However, the pathway of seeking God mounts to another level as you begin acknowledging Him and embracing the principles of His Word. There are certain answers to questions that will simply be guided by these principles. Likewise, the Lord will never lead someone to do something that violates these principles.

From the Word of God, then is derived understanding outlined in the models and pathways reflected in the biblical accounts. This is the foundation for wisdom, which involves the application of the principles from His Word. There is much that can be discerned in terms of God's will that is based on the principles of His Word and wisdom.

Then, with this foundation from God's Word and maturity, comes an additional response to righteousness and prayerfully seeking Him. This will be the recognition of that "still, small voice" or revelation from God on specific issues.

Learning to discern that still, small voice of God will establish not only your own identity in God; but your destiny. A key part in this process is gleaned from Psalm 15 where it describes the principle of "speaking truth in your own heart."

The level of interaction you have in prayer will never exceed your willingness to face the reality of who you are inwardly, despite outward facades. Psalm 51:6 describes it as the means to discern wisdom. Together with a righteous, faith-response outlined in Proverbs 3 "in all your ways acknowledge Him," the stage is set for that divine interaction or revelation in which "He shall direct your paths."

Revelation is "hearing" God on specifics. While I know ones who have heard God's audible voice, I can't say that I ever have. Those who have actually heard the audible voice of God have only done so in rare and unique situations.

The norm begins by learning to discern what scripture refers to as words of knowledge and words of wisdom, which typically come through a mental impression while reading a portion of God's Word, or a still inner voice within your own mind, that you learn to distinguish from your own thoughts. You can also "hear" from God through a specific word imparted by others. What characterizes that "hearing" is that it will always be based on the principles of God's Word and it will always flow in wisdom.

Steps to Releasing Revelation

It is important to journal, to make a record of times spent in prayer. That includes penning the questions you are asking the Lord. So, as you pray, listen and record the impressions of scripture that might come to mind, as well as the concepts regarding the specific plans you are asking the Holy Spirit to interact with you on.

From this context, begin to pray into the issues involved. As you receive impressions and words of knowledge, ask the Lord to clarify matters as you begin growing in learning to discern His "voice."

As you pray into issues, there is a tangible sequence to follow in this process to unwrap the revelation received. When revelation on a matter is received, bathe it in prayer. Test it against scripture. Ask the Lord questions. Record the impressions and review what has been journaled. Then keep saturating the unfolding revelation in prayer; until you begin gleaning illumination on the revelation.

When satisfied that sufficient illumination on the revelation has been received, then begin asking for the instruction bearing on the illumination. With the instruction will be specific direction and wisdom for steps to be taken. Again, this is a process. You need to keep the matter bathed in prayer over time which may include days or weeks, until you are satisfied with sufficient clarity on the instruction.

Once you have arrived at the point of clarity, it is time to begin asking the Lord for the timing on the release. Knowing the will of God is only part of the equation. You need to know how to apply it and when. That's why it's important, when interacting with the Holy Spirit NOT to force issues; to learn to wait before the Lord as you become proficient in this process.

The issue is usually NOT a question of hearing from the Lord. Rather, it is a tendency to get excited when you have indeed actually heard from the Lord and then to act prematurely, before getting the full picture. In other words, it's a matter of getting the full revelation, the wisdom on the application and clarity on when to act. This is a discipline that will mature and become seasoned as you learn to yield yourself in oneness with Him.

As you practice this process, it will involve a mix of writing, planning and praying as you approach alternatives to concepts being considered in the planning and decision process; but then go back and fine-tune what were first impressions as illumination and instruction become progressively clear.

More often than not, what I've written in the past for SIGN has begun with a simple word of knowledge while in prayer. As I have asked the Lord questions concerning what He was showing me, more often than not, scriptures and specific biblical and life-examples have come to mind. From that, I have written these initial impressions down and continued to pray into their significance and how they relate together. The process has begun.

Then each night as I have returned to my prayer closet, I've reviewed the revelation and impressions and begun asking the Lord where He was taking me. Very seldom, since early 1996 when SIGN was first launched, have I known where the message the Lord was giving me was going. It has unfolded, night after night while in prayer, as I've captured the wisdom and gone back and revisited the progression of concepts that have developed.

Typically, there has come a time when I have begun seeing the pattern of what has originated from the initial revelation and unfolded with illumination and eventually become a message. ONLY, after receiving the release from the Lord have I posted what's been written. There have been instances where I've developed and prayed through a theme that the Lord has told me NOT to post. Likewise, I've been amazed at how the development of the themes He has given me have fit together into the books I've written, without there ever having been an outline.

The process of hearing God on decisions or with the planning process involves a discipline of setting aside time each day to seek the Lord and then to build on the revelation and wisdom the Lord imparts over time. The time set aside should be when you are most alert and undistracted. Each person is different in terms of what time of day is best to seek the Lord. Some people are morning people; some are evening people. Seeking the Lord should come from when you are at your best.

Preparing to Receive God's Guidance

So begin by asking the Lord to speak to you and help you with the decisions or planning with which you're involved. THEN, prepare your heart. Always approach the Lord with a humble heart that is cleansed. I have developed a simple prayer that helps to push the spiritual default button and sets the stage to intentionally begin the process of hearing God. Personally, I pray this prayer as much as I find is needed and at least once a week.

> Lord God, in the Name of Your Son Jesus, I come boldly before your throne. Cleanse my heart O God. Thank You that I am cleansed by the blood of Jesus and I have invited the Holy Spirit to live within me. I bring every thought of my mind and every impression in my heart into captivity to the obedience of Jesus. Lord, I want to hear what You have to say. I trust You to communicate to me.
>
> And in the Name of Jesus, I take authority over every soulish stronghold along with every demonic and interfering spirit. I forbid any enemy activity to operate in my mind or soul. I open my heart to the Holy Spirit—to inspire, to guide, to illuminate and reveal to me truth, insights and perspectives that will anoint my efforts in this process of planning. I take authority over fear, anxiety, doubt and unbelief in the name of Jesus. I bind any negative, critical or condemning spirits in the Name of Jesus and forbid you to interfere with or in any way to imitate God's voice to me.
>
> Lord, I thank you for being in charge of every aspect of my being and for all that will unfold in this process. I look forward to growing in this new dimension with you and for what You have planned for me through it. In the Name of Jesus. Amen.

Having prepared your heart, wait quietly in His presence. As revelation begins, then write it down and begin asking the Lord to illuminate it. Begin using this process to plan and organize. It can be for an existing business or ministry, or a business or ministry that represents a dream you've had. As you plan and organize, pray into specific issues, record these planning/prayer sessions in a journal. Inquire of the Lord. Ask the Lord to connect the dots and fill in the blanks on matters not yet clear to you. Then pray some more and re-plan and re-organize. Continue the process as you take these matters before the Lord and bathe the unfolding revelation in prayer.

In the next chapter, we will employ a practical approach to planning from a Kingdom perspective. Within a community of believers, planning is a pathway of purpose strategically employing the combined gifts in a process guided by the Spirit. It is the building process with the Lord as the cornerstone and those anointed as leaders paving the way by which each one plays their part, based on the combined gifts.

Kingdom business plans are driven by stewardship and hold to a higher standard of purpose than the world's profit-model. It is a standard that if maintained, holds the potential of surpassing the profit yielded by the way of the world.

SECTION II:

PATHWAY EMPLOYING RIGHTEOUS POWER

CHAPTER 4

PRACTICAL KINGDOM PLANS

"Then David gave Solomon the plans for all that he had by the Spirit. 'All this,' said David, 'the LORD made me understand in writing, by His hand upon me, all the works of these plans '"
1 Chronicles 28:11, 12, 19

Planning maps out the pathway. It engenders the discipline and maturity needed to reach beyond the ordinary to a higher purpose.

A planning mind-set is a key factor setting leaders apart from followers. Anointed planning means the Holy Spirit is uniquely involved. When employed in conjunction with wise stewardship, it is the means by which we fulfill the mandate, to rule over the work of His hands.

Good plans begin with good planning. Good planning begins with a realistic view of the intended agenda and a big-picture grasp of and response to the times.

All plans are driven by a specific purpose. Business plans within the world are more typically based on a profit-driven model. There is no question that a business cannot endure long without a profit.

However, the mind-set for a Kingdom business is driven by stewardship and holds to a higher standard of purpose. When that standard is maintained, profit will follow; and holds the potential of surpassing the profit yielded by the profit-based model. In the Kingdom, money is neither chased nor the real goal, but instead is the servant. Kingdom planning can only be facilitated through the ongoing guidance of the Holy Spirit.

The Planning Mind-Set

With God as the Senior Partner, planning maximizes wisdom to outline goals and strategies that will serve not only the members of the enterprise, but the community served by the enterprise. It is the means by which dreams are turned into reality.

In the opening scripture from 1 Chronicles 28, we gain insight into the dynamic operating within David that was foundational to his role as a leader and king.

David planned by the Spirit. It was a cooperative process that David recorded in writing. David had a planning mind-set, but it was one that was yielded to the Lord. It was a high-level mind-set in accord with God's heart that bridged the sacred and secular, the fruit of which paved the way into a unified kingdom of God's people.

"It is the glory of God to conceal a matter, but the glory of kings is to search out a matter." Proverbs 25:2

Joseph the Patriarch also had a planning mind-set. When presented with Pharaoh's dreams, Joseph prophetically outlined the course of action that resulted in harnessing the resources of the worldly realm he was a part of, for God's redemptive purposes. In the process, Egypt was uniquely blessed.

While I have a long history of working with ones called as modern-day Josephs, much of my work in the nations is on a community level; helping to start enterprises large enough to feed a family or to support a local ministry. Three out of four of those we assist in starting a business have some type of commercially viable skill. Those remaining are individuals who might be deemed as gifted as entrepreneurs: ones who have distinct abilities to spot opportunity and turn that opportunity into profitable endeavors. In each case, dreams are turned into reality.

"Reaching to what lies ahead, I press on toward the goal for the prize of the upward call of God in Christ Jesus." Phil 3:14

Turning Dreams into Reality

Prayerful, Spirit-led plans are the means to turn dreams into reality. A good plan demands an elegant simplicity that works as well for a $100 million enterprise, as it does for a start-up entrepreneur seeking to commercialize a skill in order to feed his family. Simultaneously it requires the power to overcome the hurdles of adversity being faced.

From Asia to Israel, Africa and the Former Soviet Union, I have seen the simplicity of hand-written plans by believers willing to work and serve, become the catalyst leading to the support of their families. Likewise, serving as a pastor in many nations around the world involves congregations so poor they are unable to garner more than a meager support for their ministry. Again and again, we've seen simple plans outline the pathway by which a pastor's family, by engaging in a part-time enterprise, can not only support his or her family, but build the ministry to which they are called.

In one extremely poor Asian village, the situation was so bad that the average family was only eating one meal a day. The village was primarily Buddhist, but included three Christian families. Nothing seemed able to grow in their area, while regions a day walk away were known to be fertile. Some surmised that the area was cursed.

At one point, the Christians began praying and asking the Lord for direction. The Lord showed them that the problem was the high clay content of the soil; and that the answer would be in mobilizing an enterprise to make decorative clay pots for the West. Through prayer, initial plans were made and then with the help of connections in the West, this simple enterprise was launched. Within a three month period of time the three Christian families were eating three meals a day.

The growth of the enterprise at that juncture began opening the door to hiring other villagers. Within two years, every adult in that village was working for this simple operation and every family was eating three meals a day; and with that, this village of Buddhists had come to see the reality of God in their midst and had become followers of the One, Jesus, Whose light had turned their hunger into blessing.

Elements of the Plan

Every business plan describes certain key elements that represent stepping stones by which opportunity is identified and offered in terms of a need in the market, along with a description of basic goals and strategies to achieve the goals.

"Any enterprise is built by wise planning, becomes strong through common sense, and profits wonderfully by keeping abreast of the facts." Proverbs 24:3 TLB

Market Need. The first element of the business plan is the market need. The market need for the clay pot business was for decorative pots hung in a home that were not only attractive, but had meaning because of the story of the community who had made them, which became part of their marketing appeal.

Company Expertise and Experience. The plan needs to describe the special capabilities within the enterprise. With rich clay resources coupled with an expertise to craft attractive pots for western households, the owners quickly developed a track record of quality in the production of these items.

The Product or Service. Next is a clear description of the uniqueness of the product or service. The pots were uniquely designed with a flat backing to be hung decoratively on a wall and used as a display container for items such as flowers.

Benefits (to Customers). The plan also needs to outline the appeal or benefits the product or service has to its customers. The appeal of the clay pots was as affordable, attractive household items that carried a meaningful story about the plight of those whose hands crafted them.

The Customer. Defining the specific characteristics of primary, secondary and potential customers provides a longer-term view bearing on product development and appeals. The initial customers for the clay pots were Western gift shops, who in turn sold them to customers who displayed them in their flats and homes.

Initial Funding Requirements. In the clay pot story, initial funding requirements were almost nil (i.e. shipping, since the raw material was in abundance). For most start-ups, we recommend starting on a part-time basis with funding requirements limited to basic equipment, raw materials and advertising.

The Opportunity. The opportunity needs to be viewed in both the short-term and long-term to determine if it can be sustained over time. For the clay-pot business, the opportunity grew to the extent that it provided ongoing opportunity for this small village.

Goals and Strategies. Goals for family-based enterprises should be viewed in the context of a year. Goals should target a level of growth (i.e. sales of 400 clay pots monthly by year-end); customer-base (i.e. expand from UK gift shops to US gift shops); product-mix (i.e. household to office designs); distribution (gift shops to re-sellers); personnel (those needed to meet production/ sales goals). Each goal should have three to four strategies as the means to accomplish the goal.

Annual Sales and Budget. Annual sales are simply the monthly projection of sales expected over a year's time frame. They are expressed in income for each month and will be tied to the expanding monthly expense requirements to establish sufficient operating capital to maintain the momentum of the growth.

Vision as a Community Builder. Together with the Lord as the Senior Partner in the operation, the community builder vision will differentiate the Kingdom business. The community builder vision, beyond being a good witness of the Lord, is the means by which the business proactively will bless the community it serves. In the clay pot story, it demonstrated the reality of God by raising the standard of living in the village so that the entire village was no longer hungry.

Planning by the Spirit

Like King David, we can make a difference when we plan by the Spirit. By interactive prayer and the application of our gifts we enter a cooperative process with the Lord. David recorded what he gleaned from the Spirit in writing. David had a planning mind-set yielded to the Lord.

Good planning by the Spirit helps you avoid frequent mistakes made in starting a new business, which include:

- Being under-capitalized; taking on too much debt
- Making unrealistic goals
- Lack of good accounting and money management
- Lack of sound advice and wisdom
- Inadequate operating capital
- Haste and impulsiveness
- Using prayer or God as an after-thought.

Practical plans consider the options and map out a pathway of progress. A practical Kingdom plan will organize your thinking and clarify prudent steps. It will consider the key elements in anticipating alternatives and decisions to be made. Ongoing prayed-through planning will help you manage change and avoid pitfalls. It will uncover opportunity and unveil timing issues. It will open doors.

"The plans of the diligent lead to plenty, but everyone who is hasty to poverty." Proverbs 21:5

Ongoing planning, with the Lord as your Senior Partner, enables you to operate within the real world of your market. It is a realistic means of staying in touch with your customers. It helps anticipate the strategies of competition. It likewise provides the wisdom for realistic marketing communication strategies to attract and maintain new customers.

In short, at the core of running a business is the art of managing change. Holy Spirit planning enables you to manage change so that change works for you, as you realistically approach and maximize opportunity.

"Be diligent to know the state of your flocks and attend to your herds." Prov 27:23

To enhance the Kingdom dimension needed to operate in tough spiritual environments, our entrepreneurial program sets up groups of 5 to 15 members led by spiritually mature persons experienced in business ownership. These groups, to be explained in more detail in a Chapter 10, serve the purposes of accountability, prayer-support, and practical wisdom into the planning developments among its members. In short, they are a hybrid of spiritual mentoring and business incubators.

The Kingdom Dynamic and Righteous Power

The clay pot story is a good example of dominion; of God's people employing righteous power in ruling over the work of His hands. The cooperative effort between the believers responding to what God showed them brought them into a dynamic that not only met their needs, but enabled them to be blessed to be a blessing as they extended the opportunity of the blessing to their neighbors.

Again, a Kingdom business is driven by stewardship and holds to a higher standard of purpose than worldly businesses. That standard goes beyond being a light to the community by proactively using the unique capabilities of the business dynamic as a means to extend the "blessing" and build community.

"I am the Lord your God, who teaches you to profit, Who leads you in the way you should go." Isaiah 48:17

So it is that learning to discern God's direction and wisdom for our individual lives, for a congregation, for a business or for a community is developed through the proactive process of seeking Him, then mapping out a practical plan to follow.

Within a community of believers, planning is a pathway of purpose strategically employing the diversity of gifts in a process guided by the Spirit. It is the building process with the Lord as the cornerstone and those anointed as leaders paving the way by which each one plays their part, as they enter a realm, unparalleled by the world around them, of being blessed to be a blessing.

In the next chapter, we will take a closer look at what it takes to enter God's economy. God did not make his people to follow the way of the world, but rather the other way around: to be a light to the world. It involves the pathway of the Kingdom and the operation of God's economy.

CHAPTER 5

ENTERING GOD'S ECONOMY

"For the secret things belong to the LORD, but those that are revealed belong to us and to our children forever."
Deuteronomy 29:29

God did not make His people to be like everyone else; nor to follow a methodology embraced by a corrupt and compromising world. Instead, He has unveiled everything needed for those known by His name to be the head and not the tail. It all begins with the choice to enter the narrow path of the Kingdom and His economy.

In Deuteronomy 29:29 above, Moses reveals the insight that has made the Jewish people to be the most remarkable people in history. When the Jewish people have gotten it right, the bottom line is that the Lord and His principles have been their foundation not only as individuals, but as a people. In Isaiah 43 it is revealed that the Lord chose them as a witness to understand that He is God.

God's economy is not some new dimension of Western Christian pop-culture. It is the dimension of those "secret things" that has been an integral part of the model explaining why the Jewish people have not only survived the civilizations that have come and gone over the centuries, but have been disproportionate contributors to the advancement of those societies.

As already explained in previous chapters, the model for these secret things came from Abraham, who operated a God-centered, entrepreneurial community. The mantle also came from Abraham: "to be blessed to be a blessing." Moses then recorded the principles comprehensively for the operation of the model and mandate in the Books of Moses. Entrepreneurship is the spark that both ignites and fuels this dynamic encompassing the model and mandate that we refer to as God's economy.

The Distinguishing Dynamic

The intertwining dimensions of God's economy and entrepreneurship are reflected in the story of Isaac in Genesis 26. It was a time of famine, but the Lord told Isaac that He would override the curse impacting those in that land and bless him. So Isaac obeyed the Lord and sowed in a land where nothing was growing. The result was against the odds of adversity, as his efforts brought increase to the level that scripture describes: as Isaac "prospered and continued to prosper until he became very prosperous."

In the process, God's blessing upon Isaac distinguished and made him a light to societies who were struggling around him. God's economy thrives when God's people hear the voice of the Lord and obey, despite the circumstances of adversity.

In 2008, I was asked to conduct one of my God's economy entrepreneurial workshops in an area of Asia where people of faith were being persecuted. I was told what I presented would be for a group of existing business owners interested in pressing beyond the superficialities in doing business God's way.

I was stunned when I arrived, to find that ALL of the 38 business-owners were pastors and assistant pastors. One by one the Lord had been uniquely speaking to them and leading them to start their own businesses. In each case, they not only succeeded in their efforts with their small enterprises, which amazingly still allowed them ample time for their pastoral responsibilities; but they had become an example to their congregations and a witness to the authorities, who no longer viewed them as poor, non-contributors to the community.

At the onset of imparting our program's principles to these pastors, the Lord gave me a word of wisdom for them from 1 Peter 2:15: "That by their good works, they were putting to silence the ignorance of foolish men." Indeed, through the Abrahamic model and the mantle of being blessed to be a blessing, God was making them the head and not the tail and giving them *influence* in their communities, where they previously had been despised and scorned.

Both God's economy and entrepreneurship are driven by that feature of His nature, which is creative and brings increase. God's economy and entrepreneurship are each based on a people who serve as leaders, not as the world views leadership, but through *influence*. The bottom line to God's economy and entrepreneurship is power; but again not like the world conceives of power, but instead the righteous power that overcomes evil with good, when His people operate in oneness with Him.

Entering God's Economy

Entrance into God's economy is based on certain principles. These biblical dynamics extend beyond good ethics and represent the foundation to God's economy. They include an interaction of the following key factors:

Trust in the Lord. The sequence in Proverbs 3:5,6 indicates that the natural response to decisions and mapping out future plans is drawn from our own understanding. Yet, it admonishes us NOT to lean on our own understanding, but to give first priority to our trust in the Lord. To do so will take faith and it will require reaching for both the wisdom and revelation that mark the ones guided by His Spirit.

Priestly-King Role. Abraham, Joseph and David are examples of the heroes of faith who served in priestly-king roles. They each were planners who changed the course of the world within their spheres, as leaders whose distinctive was being led by the Spirit of the Lord. For each, they made an impact through God before ascending to positions that gave them higher-level platforms to accomplish God's strategic purposes. The dynamic of God's economy will become a reality for those who trust the Lord and operate with a king's heart, regardless of the level of the position.

Kingdom Principles. The Kingdom of God is driven by different principles than those of the world. Foremost is that God is actively sought and involved. Employing righteous power in worldly settings will seem as a paradox to the way the world operates and succeeds; but is ultimately far more enduring and liberating.

Dominion. Understanding the authority we wield as God's ambassadors is at the heart of ruling over the work of His hands. So it is with God's economy. We establish God's authority within the economic sphere as a key part of being a light to the communities around us, as we are blessed to be a blessing.

Small Beginnings. Growth will come from humble beginnings for those who are diligent with what they've been entrusted. Enterprises birthed as Kingdom initiatives need to be started at a level in which we get the "God as Senior Partner" dimension down before growth comes and things become more complicated. In other words, when learning to trust in the Lord as priestly-kings in ruling over the work of His hands, we need to walk before we run; regardless and perhaps in spite of the position one may have come from in the world's structure. That means it is not what we can do for God, but rather what we allow Him to do through us.

"If you have run with footmen and they have wearied you, then how can you contend with horses? If in the land of peace in which you trusted, they wearied you then how will you do in the floodplain of the Jordan?" Jeremiah 12:5

Stewardship, Faith and Multiplication. Stewardship, faith and multiplication are uniquely correlated within God's economic system. When Joseph was a slave in Potiphar's house, Genesis 39 tells us that "everyone saw that the Lord was with Joseph and made ALL he did to prosper." Joseph's results demonstrated something more that even the non-believing Egyptians could only conclude came from Joseph's God. Despite his loss of freedom, Joseph's identity was in God and he was a good steward, with all he did being committed to the Lord, with God then bringing blessings upon him that blessed those he served.

Perseverance. A key dimension of faith is the waiting period needed to overcome the hurdles and bring forth the fruit. Within God's economy this will vary depending on the initiative. In case after case of businesses we have helped in persecuted lands, we have seen remarkable things happen, that could only be explained by God, when God is made Senior Partner and the pathway for the plan is committed to Him.

We encourage these entrepreneurs to look for simple milestones that mark the progress of the process. When simple beginnings begin to see enough customers that growth is evident; that is a milestone. When the influence of a business starts to demonstrate the reality of God; then an important milestone is passed.

Generosity. Jewish tradition upholds the community goal of being self-sufficient. Jesus' admonition that you'll be in the world, but not of the world conforms to this principle. It operates through a combination of nurturing the success of its members, with care being given to NOT becoming dependent on the world's system through its own network of enterprise and the dynamic explained by the Hebrew word tz'dakah. Typically tz'dakah is translated as righteousness, but it literally means charitable righteousness and is a community dynamic that basically is proactive, planned generosity that multiplies the benefit to the entire community.

Unity. Unity is not blind conformity, but rather the mutual, trust-effort of all the members seeking common goals to the benefit of all. Again and again within the Books of Moses is the admonition of fairness in the application of righteous power with the expectation of benefit between brethren within the community; with the motivator "so that the Lord your God may bless the work of your hands." Unity is released when the members are working toward the common good.

Work. The operative word for work in Hebrew today is avodah. To glean insight into Hebrew words, one first looks at its root; and then the correlated words that share that root. The root for avodah means "to witness." The key words that share this root are "passion," "purpose" and "future." There is no connection between avodah and the Hebrew word for toil. In God's economy, work indeed should be one's passion, through which we have a purpose and attain a future.

God's economy is more than faith in God. It is cooperation with God by means of His principles for His purposes. It's released when we rule over the work of His hands in serving His purposes and people. Even then it far exceeds the issue of good ethics, as we adhere to the voice of the Lord with Him serving as our Senior Partner.

"Lord, what is man, that You take thought of him? Yet You have made him a little lower than God. You crown him with glory and majesty and have made him to rule over the works of Your hands."
Psalm 8:6

The Application of God's Economy

With the entrance into God's economy a seed is planted. It is the seed of the Kingdom, like that of a mustard seed that Jesus used to illustrate how the Kingdom of God manifests and grows.

God's economy is an outworking of the Kingdom that, like the mustard seed, which is the smallest or least likely of all the seeds; will grow beyond that of the other plants and herbs of the field. Its disproportionate growth potential is to become as a tree that houses added-value dimensions illustrated by *"even the birds of the air nesting in its branches."* God's economy is like that seed, as it is the expression of righteous power that breaks the bondage of corruption.

One of the Asian pastors we helped into a self-supporting role cheaply purchased a failed roadside, breakfast noodle shop in his community. It had failed because it didn't have enough customers to cover its expenses. Despite that, the Lord gave this outgoing pastor a strong word on acquiring this small operation.

Because his Christian activities, which included birthing seven congregations in the region and training up pastors for each, periodically attracted local authorities, resulting in interrogations and beatings; locals who didn't know him were curious and began stopping into his shop. Within two weeks, he, his wife and mother who ran this enterprise doubled the amount of noodle dishes sold at its start and were meeting their expenses. Within a few months, for the few morning hours this shop was open, he was supporting his family AND bringing new believers into the fold.

Interlink Business, Ministry and Community. Jesus used the platform of Peter's fishing boat as a means to teach the people. It was a unique way by which the foundation of Peter's business simultaneously served the purpose of ministry and blessed the community. It was an interlinking of business and ministry.

"Stepping into one of the boats, Jesus asked Simon its owner to push out into the water. So he sat in the boat and taught the people." Luke 5:2,3

The Edge: Supernatural Faith. The supernatural faith required to enter God's economy carries an ongoing expectation and must be continuous, as God always provides an advantage that will come from "being about His business." When Jesus completed His teaching (Luke 5), he told Peter to throw out his nets. Peter quibbled, saying he'd been fishing there all night with no catch, but then he obeyed and the scripture says the nets became so full of fish that they began to tear.

So it happened when Isaac obeyed God and sowed in famine in Genesis 26. So it was with the Asian pastor who opened a failed noodle shop that eventually became a small community gathering place. The edge is in applying supernatural faith for both entering and in maintaining this realm that interlinks business and ministry.

Extend Charity (Tz'dakah) and Reciprocity. God's economy flourishes on tz'dakah, the community dynamic of reciprocal generosity that pivots on the mantle of Abraham to be blessed to be a blessing. Reciprocity is reaping what you sow. When this type of community generosity is in operation, it is a mark of the spiritual maturity of its members.

One of our dear friends I have worked with in mobilizing African entrepreneurs is an executive for a Kingdom operation in Africa. His passion is giving. He looks for opportunities to be a meaningful blessing. His conclusion is that every major opportunity that has come to his operation has been the result of his obedience in giving.

"Jesus said, 'give and it will be given unto you, good measure, pressed down, shaken together and running over. For with the measure you use, it will be measured back to you." Luke 6: 38

"The generous soul will be made rich, and he who waters will also be watered." Proverbs 11:29

Expect the Result of Faith, Diligence and Multiplication. God's economy is not for the slovenly, the slothful or presumptuous. It takes diligence. It takes a heart that is constantly seeking God and willing to act in faith at God's guidance. From faith and diligence will come the release of that dimension of God's nature within those who believe: to create, innovate, build and multiply. From God's guidance will come righteous power to bring increase and nurture profit God's way (Isaiah 48:17).

"The hand of the diligent shall rule, for diligence is man's precious possession." Prov 12:26

"Promotion comes neither from the east nor the west, but from the Lord." Psalm 75:6

Exercise Servant Leadership. Entrance into God's economy as an operative part of His Kingdom requires the employment of righteous power. This is the power entrusted to those who God prepares to be the head and not the tail; to those willing to pay the cost to exercise servant leadership.

"The king of the Gentiles lords over them; and those who have authority over them are called benefactors. But not so with you;

let him who is the greatest become the least, and the leader as the servant." Luke 22:25-27

"You crown him with glory and majesty and have made him to rule over the works of Your hands." Psalm 8:6

Assume Community Responsibility. Leadership in God's economy begins by assuming community responsibility. This is the responsibility of the mature that rises above self and is other-directed. Community responsibility that employs righteous power is the dynamic that the world living under the bondage of corruption is seeking as we demonstrate the reality of God operating within our spheres, as we are blessed to be a blessing.

"Unto him that much is given, much is required; and to whom men have committed much, of him they will ask the more." Luke 12:48

"For creation itself longs for the revealing of the sons of God that it might be delivered from the bondage of corruption as it gains entrance into this glorious freedom." Romans 8:19-21

In the next chapter, we will take a closer look at the dynamic of entrepreneurship, as God intended it to operate within the community of His people. In that context, it operates as both an individual and a community factor of the "secret things" revealed by God to His own that is key to being the head and not the tail, as we apply the model and the mandate. As a true expression of righteous power, entrepreneurship is both the spark and fuel that drives God's economy.

CHAPTER 6

BIBLICAL ENTREPRENEURSHIP AND SUCCESS

*"She considers a field and buys it. Out of her earnings
she plants a vineyard. She sees that her trading is profitable
and her lamp does not go out at night."*
Proverbs 31:16-18

Entrepreneurship, as most people think of it, is generally lumped into a vague category of anything-to-do with business. Yet, it's more, so very much more.

My perspectives on entrepreneurship, aside from being a business owner, have been influenced by two primary sources. First, is the Word of God. Second is by a dear friend who is considered a world-class expert and practitioner on the topic.

Bill Bolton, committed Christian and former tentmaker in the Sudan, as well as being founder of the St. John Innovation Centre of St. John's College at Cambridge University is co-author (along with John Thompson) of the best book I've been exposed to on the subject. It's titled *"Entrepreneur: Talent, Temperament and Technique."* The Bolton-Thompson definition for an entrepreneur is: "a person who habitually creates and innovates to build something of value around perceived opportunity."

The Bolton-Thompson definition succinctly conforms to the entrepreneurial description outlined in the opening scripture. The most excellent woman of Proverbs 31 is clearly an entrepreneur.

Biblical Entrepreneurship

These three short verses point to one who is able to spot opportunity and is carefully decisive. She makes her assets work for her. As a good steward, she knows how to bring about increase and innovatively creates earnings through what she does with what she has. She provides a good service that serves a clientele, at a profit. Finally, she is diligent in the ongoing process of managing and leveraging opportunity.

Women do tend to make good entrepreneurs. If business employs the art of managing change, then entrepreneurship is the art of identifying and developing opportunity. As my fiend Dr. Bolton notes in the title of his book, entrepreneurship incorporates a talent/ a gift; a temperament; and it is definitely a technique that can be developed.

A key part of God's nature is to create and bring increase. These factors are vital components of entrepreneurship. As His nature resides within those who believe, there is a certain level at which this entrepreneurial dimension works within each believer. For some it operates as a natural gift. For others, it represents an enhancement to other forms of giftings, such as the anointed gift of Bezalel in Exodus. Within community, biblical entrepreneurship represents a potential to be nurtured as will be explained in Chapter 10.

"See, I have called by name Bezalel. I have filled him with the Spirit of God in wisdom, in understanding, in knowledge, and in all kinds of craftsmanship, to make artistic designs..." Exodus 31:2-6

Entrepreneurship as God intended is designed to thrive within the community of His people. It is both an individual and a community factor of the "secret things" revealed by God to His own, designed to play a key role in them becoming the head and not the tail. As a true expression of righteous power, it can change the spiritual climate as it demonstrates the reality of God to non-believers.

I've mentioned in a previous chapter that roughly three out of four of those of the persecuted church for whom we help start self-sustaining enterprises do so based by commercializing a skill they possess. The remaining ratio are ones with a natural gift as an entrepreneur; who are able to spot opportunity and know what to do about it.

This subtle opportunity dynamic differs significantly from the misconception, often held in the West that starting a successful enterprise is based on conceiving and developing a better "mouse trap." This is a much riskier approach. Success of a new startup takes not only an expertise, but a realistic response to market need. In God's economy, the success ratio is driven by much more, as I will soon discuss, not the least of which is making God the Senior Partner and clearly adhering to His guidance.

Transforming the Spiritual Climate

One of the attendees in our God's economy program was a tribal leader from a poor Asian village. He was both a pastor and leader of this tribal village. The entire village was comprised of committed believers. Their minority status and poverty, along with their faith in God, all seemed to intensify the level of persecution they received from local authorities. When roads and electrical service were washed out by a storm, the authorities didn't bother restoring either. In the surrounding villages were other believers; minority, tribal groups treated in much the same way.

Upon completion of our training, I learned that this pastor had an expertise and experience in breeding and raising a particular variety of pig, considered a delicacy in his culture, within urban upscale restaurants. So we helped him with the purchase of three of these valuable, fast-breeding pigs.

Eighteen months later we made a visit to this rural village to observe first-hand what had developed since helping put this man into business. We were met not only by this man, who partook of our training, but four other pastors from surrounding villages. What we learned was that from the first group of piglets, this pastor not only made some profitable sales that began supporting his family AND his ministry, but he trained two other pastors in his skill and gave them each pigs to breed. He did the same thing for two additional tribal leaders with the next group of new piglets.

So, not only did he begin the turnaround for his own village with his simple business, but he set up four other pastors in business who also began experiencing God's blessings upon their villages and congregations from the fruit of true biblical community and entrepreneurship. From the noticeable change taking place within this pastor's village, authorities finally restored their power and roads.

The Entrepreneurial Dynamic

Entrepreneurs are people who do things that make a difference. They create, build and are at the heart of change in society. In most cases, they are ordinary people with special matching talents and temperaments. Entrepreneurs spot opportunity and know what to do about it. In short, an entrepreneur is one who:

- Can deliver on what they say they will do,
- Knows what opportunities to go for,
- Demonstrates the creativity and ideas that can't be stopped in the first place,
- Operates as a team player and has a purpose that serves.

One of many nuggets I've gleaned from Professor Bolton comes from a study conducted by Jill Garrett, former CEO of the Gallup organization in the UK. In a study of leaders of successful organizations, she concluded that these leaders could do "something" better than 10,000 other people. That "something" was a developed-gift in each leader. In other words, most people have their own unique gift. (See Chapter 2)

Not unlike an accomplished musician or sports person, what differentiates the successful from the mediocre is in the level in which the gift is developed. In business, it's developing the gift to be commercialized, while linking it up with the market need. Then wisdom shapes the mind-set that accompanies this "gift."

Institutional versus Entrepreneurial Mind-Sets

Keen insight into the entrepreneurial approach to business was outlined by John Skully in his book *"Odyssey: Pepsi to Apple."* Mr. Skully was the man behind the 80's soft drink advertising campaign known as the Pepsi Challenge in which Pepsi made major inroads into Coke's market share.

Then one day his good friend Steve Jobs (an inveterate entrepreneur) at Apple Computer challenged Skully (a hardened institutional practitioner) with the words: "Do you want to peddle sugared water for the rest of your life or do you want to change the world?" So Skully accepted the offer made by Steve Jobs to take over as president of Apple. It was culture shock and devastating for both Skully and Apple's engrained entrepreneurial foundations for doing business.

Jobs eventually took back the reins of running Apple. However, the experience awakened Skully to the operating dynamics of a corporate culture and way of thinking that was entrepreneurial rather than that of his institutional mind-set.

Taking a bit of license in summarizing his insights, the main focus for the institutional mind-set is on the organization; while entrepreneurial thinking is more on the individual. The institutional structure is tighter and more controlling than the entrepreneurial. For the most part, innovation in the institution serves to reduce risk; whereas entrepreneurially, it is to manage risk and opportunity, which fits more closely to the interaction of faith and risk in a Kingdom setting. The ability sought in an institution gives focus to managing the status quo; whereas entrepreneurially it is the ability to embrace and adapt to change.

The expected output for the institutional mind-set is market-share, whereas the entrepreneur thinks more in terms of market creation. In an institution, leadership tends to reflect a micro-managing orientation, whereas entrepreneurially the leadership focus is on motivating and nurturing. For the institutional mind-set, the product is a service or artifact. For the one who thinks like an entrepreneur, the product is a dream. Finally, the typical motivation for the institutional thinker is to make money, whereas for the entrepreneurial thinker, it is to make history.

God-Centered Community Entrepreneurs

With these insights into the mind-set of an entrepreneur, God-centered community entrepreneurs are in touch with customers and the community they serve. Like the Asian pastor who helped other village pastors set up their businesses, God's entrepreneurs grasp the big picture and overriding need of the common good. Simultaneously, as they let their Light shine, they build bridges with the broader community. In all that they do, they adhere to God's guidance. They are generous and participate in purposeful community gatherings that engender unity. Their response to customers and community is gratefulness. They understand reciprocity and know what it means to "give back" in the process of making a difference in their community.

God-centered community entrepreneurs are models of operating with fairness, excellence, honesty and accountability. As good stewards and witnesses, they are spiritually and socially responsible, proactively serving others with the mantle of Abraham as they are blessed to be a blessing.

The Entrepreneur Challenge and Imperative

The responsibility of God's entrepreneurs is stressed by Dr. Bolton, who articulates the entrepreneur challenge and imperative. The point bears on the biblical theme of employing righteous power in a corrupt world with truth, serving and influence; thereby making a difference.

Many years ago, a man by the name of Machiavelli was at the opposite extreme in terms of the use of power. He wrote a short book on the devious use of power titled *"The Prince."* Yet within his treatise, was the profound statement underscoring the entrepreneurial dynamic: *"There is nothing more difficult to conduct or more uncertain in its success than to take the lead in a new order of things."*

Entrepreneurs are ones who thrive on challenge, uncertainty and chaos. As a part of the leaders sent to spy out the Promised Land, Joshua and Caleb responded as God's entrepreneurs with faith, not fear. Their comrade's report was of them being as grasshoppers in the sight of the giants in the land. Instead of the grasshopper mindset, Joshua and Caleb saw both the opportunity and God's intention for His people.

Entrepreneurs challenge the status quo; they spot opportunity and turn it into a new order of things. God's highest priorities will always come through His "people" operating in community; cooperating with God, by means of their combined gifts to bring change

that advances the Kingdom of God. Both the challenge and imperative for God's entrepreneurs is the responsibility to identify your
unique sphere and enter that calling to be blessed to be a blessing;
and by so doing, changing the spiritual climate.

The Faith-Gift of God's Increase

Being blessed to be a blessing sets in motion God's faith-gift
of increase. To create, build, bring increase and multiply are key
dimensions of God's nature. These dynamics are also at the heart of
entrepreneurship.

Operating on this level begins by embracing a generous, giving
heart. Generosity and stewardship in God's economy operate in
tandem. That means not only managing your money well, but always
being in control of your assets and income instead of allowing them
to control you. The next point to participating in this flow of the
faith-gift of increase is to learn to leverage opportunity and change.
This goes back to the foundations outlined in the chapters on planning. From these dynamics will come a process that will yield
enlargement and multiplication.

Success Principles for Biblical Entrepreneurs

In God's economy the measures of success differ widely from
those of the world. The world's focus is generally on money, pres-
tige and power. In the book of Isaiah we capture a succinct glimpse
of God's perspective for each of these factors:

*"Then the fool will no longer be called generous, nor the miser
said to be bountiful. The schemes of the schemer are evil; devising
wicked plans to destroy the poor with lying words, despite the needy
speaking justice. The generous man devises generous plans, and by
generosity he shall stand."* Isaiah 32: 5-8

The measure of biblical success, as is its pathway, employs righteous power to be blessed in order to extend the blessing. A few key
biblical principles tied to God's pathway for success include:

Learn the art of diligence. Diligence is a precious possession that will lead to an excellence and authority that contributes to the common good.

"The hand of the diligent will rule." Proverbs 12:24

Become excellent at something you do. The mastery of a gift/ a skill that serves will bring about not only purpose, but the recognition of its significance for the benefit of the community.

"Do you see a man who excels in his work, he will stand before kings." Proverbs 22:29

Assume responsibility and manage detail. Assuming responsibility means managing the way you make a difference down to the details, not only in bringing blessing upon yourself but in that next step of being a blessing to others.

"Be diligent to know the state of your flocks and attend to your herds." Proverbs 27:23

Strive for trustworthiness and dependability. Being worthy of trust begins in our own hearts with the way we make a lifestyle of the generous and dependable extension of our gifts to help others.

"He who walks with integrity and works righteousness and speaks truth in his heart... who swears to his own hurt and does not change." Psalm 15:2-4

Treat your customers like family. In business, when dealing with issues of customer service and marketing, the most strategic, yet most subtle thing that can be done is to build genuine relationships through treating customers like family

"A good name is to be chosen over great riches, loving favor than silver and gold. By humility and fear of the Lord are riches and honor and life." Proverbs 22:1,4

Discipline yourself to view things from a long-term perspective. Wisdom pays the cost in prioritizing and pacing the development of an enterprise. Reach for more, but be willing to be faithful in the small things on a stable pathway to the future.

"Prepare your outside work, make it fit for yourself in the field; and afterward build your house." Proverbs 24:27

"Little by little will you drive them out from before you, until you have increased and are numerous enough to take possession of the land." Exodus 23:30; Deuteronomy 7:22

Be alert for opportunities for ownership. Beginning in the books of Moses, the Bible emphasizes the value of private ownership by which opportunity is leveraged.

"She considers a field and buys it; out of her earnings she plants a vineyard." Proverbs 31:16

Learn to manage risk. Faith and risk operate hand in hand. Responding to God's guidance will involve getting out of our comfort zones and the management of risk.

"Against all hope, Abraham believed God." Romans 4:18

Make your assets work for you. Foundational to ruling over the work of His hands is the stewardship that brings increase to that with which we're entrusted.

"Well done, good and faithful servant. You were faithful over a few things, I will make you ruler over many things." Matthew 25:18

Surround yourself with wise counselors. The emphasis is on *wisdom* drawn from the "experience" of those who have expertise in the pathway you're walking.

"In the multitude of counselors there is safety." Proverbs 11:14; 24:6

Make decisions based on the right thing to do. The world confuses stewardship with squeezing everything possible out of a deal. In contrast, in the Books of Moses is the principle of gleaning, of leaving something for the less fortunate at harvest time.

"What does the Lord require of you but to do justly, and to love kindness and mercy, and to humble yourself and walk humbly with your God." Micah 6:8

Make the Lord your Senior Partner. Biblical success will pivot on the level at which God's guidance is sought and accurately adhered to.

"Seek first His Kingdom and righteousness and all these other things will be added to you." Matthew 6:33

Your God-Centered Entrepreneurial Agenda

Your God-centered entrepreneurial agenda is your calling, your destiny. It begins by seeking to know God's heart and his priorities for you. It incorporates a progressive grasp of applying the biblical mantle of being blessed in order to be a blessing. That involves identifying your mix of "gifts" and personal sphere of influence, along with the authority from the anointing that you have to bring multiplication.

This form of multiplication involves replicating your efforts; extending and enabling opportunity to others through proactive mentoring. In this way you will fulfill your God-centered entrepreneurial agenda or calling by ruling over the work of your hands as a cooperative process with the Lord at the helm.

SECTION III:

MATURITY AS A BODY

CHAPTER 7

STEWARDSHIP
IN GOD'S ECONOMY

"To the steward who brought increase he said, well done,
good and faithful servant. You were faithful over a few things,
I will make you ruler over many."
Matthew 25:18

The parable of the talents addresses stewardship. The expectation is to manage whatever resources we've been assigned each according to his own ability, and then to bring increase. The servant who was afraid and hid his assets in order not to lose anything was not only judged, but judged as being wicked. Why?

The answer lies within the dynamics that incorporate the model, the mandate and mantle (see Chapter 1) God designed for His people. Those known by His Name have been entrusted with a power and authority. It is a righteous power and authority that distinguishes us from the world.

As such, we are not called to be or to operate like "everyone else." As God's people, we are called to be distinctive, to operate at a higher standard. Scripture tells us that the wisdom of Daniel was ten times better than the best the worldly advisors in the king's court could offer.

Since God has had a people, those known by His Name have been a light to the surrounding societies because of God being with them. Within a fallen world, described by scripture as ruled by the bondage of corruption, the story of God's people has again and again been one of breaking the constraints of this bondage that grips the world; and directs the way it thinks and employs power. Those called by God's name have a mandate to exercise righteous power, to overcome evil with good, and as the head and not the tail, to rule over the works of His hands.

In short, we're called to steward not only our individual gifts, but as a people to make a difference in the world around us through our active participation in the model that drives God's economy and the mantle of being blessed to be a blessing.

The Mind-Set and Process

When approaching stewardship within God's economy, it's important to have a resource mind-set rather than a focus restricted to the monetary. The monetary will be there, but the monetary is only a part of the equation and needs to be the servant rather than the end-purpose, as the bigger-picture is engaged in an interaction of human, financial, community and spiritual capital and resources.

Balanced stewardship of establishing God's Kingdom rule and authority involves daily communication and cooperation with God, as His stewards. Within that context is the mandate of God's people to establish His authority described from Genesis to Revelation as dominion.

Foundational to this mandate is a mature grasp of God's Word and of hearing and obeying His voice. It is a process that evolves over time for both individuals and generations that employs the model that merges the spiritual in building community through the dynamic of God's economy. The result of this process applied is the reversal of the bondage of corruption and the establishment of God's Kingdom rule. The process of stewarding this mandate and mantle employs strategic ways of thinking and operating.

Discipline and Diligence. The hallmarks for the stewardship for spiritual maturity, leadership and a genuine role in God's economy are disciple and diligence. They go hand-in-hand. Discipline and diligence yield fruitfulness. Proverbs 16:32 reveals that: "The one who rules his own spirit is mightier than he who takes a city."

Stewardship reflects the focus of diligence that results in excellence.

"Be diligent to know the state of your flocks and attend to your herds." Proverbs 27: 21

Your Calling and Sphere. It's important to accurately grasp and wield what one has been called to do. However, that grasp must be combined with the humility and wisdom of being a faithful steward within the context of the sphere of authority functioning at a given time. Joseph the Patriarch served within his sphere of authority he had as a slave in Potiphar's house and then as a prisoner. Those steps of stewardship were significant to opening the doors of opportunity to him being called before Pharaoh.

"A man's gift makes room for him and brings him before great men." Proverbs 18:16

"But we will not boast beyond measure, but within the sphere which God has appointed to us." 2 Corinthians 10:13

A Hedge against the World's System. Hedges against a dependency on the world's system range from being debt-free and self-sustaining private business ownership, to creating a resource cushion beyond the system.

"You will be in the world, but not of the world." John 17:15, 16

An Eye for Value. The process of stewardship requires an eye for value, in both what you offer and what you acquire. Developing excellence carries the requirement for an eye for value for the things that drive the uniqueness of a particular business.

Wisdom in Priorities. The wise steward pays the costs in prioritizing agendas in the process of building a business and serving the community.

"Prepare your outside work, make it fit for yourself in the field; and afterward build your house." Proverbs 24: 27

God imparts information, wisdom and insights to His covenant people. The process involves faithfulness in taking care of what you already have and investing in not only improving efficiencies, but the skills required in key functions.

"Thus says the Lord, 'I am the Lord your God who teaches you to profit, who leads you by the way you should go." Isaiah 48:17

Alert to Business Cycles. Just as there are cycles and seasons in nature, so there are cycles in business. Some of these cycles are unique to an industry; some are driven by fiscal issues at governmental policy levels. In each case, the wise steward understands and is prepared for the changes in business cycles. Understanding the cycles is key to expansion.

"I know how to be abased and I know how to abound." Philippians 4:11

The Dynamics of Stewardship
Stewardship within God's economy begins by fully embracing the Lord as your Senior Partner. Again, that involves actively seeking His guidance on decisions based on a mature wisdom of the truths found in the Word of God. It also involves mentoring and minyan-style support group participation which will be discussed in Chapter 10.

"The earth is the Lord's and all of its fullness, the world and those that dwell therein." Psalm 24:1

As junior partners, our stewardship involves the management and increase of the resources noted in the opening scripture with which, in each of our spheres, we are entrusted.

"The silver and gold is Mine, says the Lord of Hosts." Haggai 2:8

The key dynamics of stewardship in God's economy include
* The faith-gift of sowing and reaping
* Managing money and resources
* Bringing increase.

Sowing and Reaping

In God's economy, stewardship begins with a generous heart that puts into practice what scripture describes as "sowing and reaping."

The dynamic of sowing and reaping begins with understanding that God is the source of our supply. He is the one we depend on; not a job, nor the world's economy. Isaac sowed in famine because God told him to and against the odds, he prospered.

"My God shall provide all your need according to His riches in Glory." Philippians 4:19

So, by first acknowledging God as the source of all increase, we then sow by giving. Again, the mind-set should extend beyond simply the monetary, to include our time, our gifts and our wisdom.

"Give and it will be given unto you, good measure pressed down, shaken together and running over, shall men give into your bosom. For with the same measure that you mete, it will be measured to you again." Luke 6:38

As we first look to God as our source and are generous with what we have to give, we can then expect His intervention in bringing increase.

"Ask and it will be given to you; seek and you will find; knock and the door will be opened." Luke 11:9

"I have planted, Apollos watered, but God gave the increase." 1 Corinthians 3:6

One of the more successful business people we have had opportunity to work with in persecuted lands told us an amazing testimony.

At the time he met the Lord, he was so poor, that he didn't even have a bicycle, which is considered a sub-standard mode of transportation in his society. Someone gave him a Bible. In his initial reading of the Word of God, he was gripped by the truth in Genesis 12 that God would bless those who blessed Israel. From the meager, piecemeal work he had at the time, he began giving to his congregation AND to a ministry in Israel.

Within three months, he had a new, full-time job. So he increased his sowing. From his new job, he learned a new skill and three years later, he started his own business. He worked hard at his new business and took great joy in sharing the increase with the poor, his congregation and opportunities for blessing the believers in Israel. Five years after the start of his business, he has crews of people working for him and not only owns his own home, but has helped build a home for his pastor.

Another unique story about sowing and reaping involves a man whose testimony began during WWII. Robert LeTourneau, committed Christian and business owner, began having unusual dreams that he began to discern were from the Lord. These dreams outlined designs for a new mode of earth-moving equipment.

This man of God captured what God was showing him and began manufacturing these new designs of earth-moving equipment. Their implementation was used to build runways on military airbases in the Pacific that accelerated construction ten times faster than previous equipment, giving the Allies a significant advantage.

Robert LeTourneau went on to become renowned for his generosity in the support of an array of Christian initiatives. It began when he made the decision to increase his faithfulness in tithing to a level of 25 percent. When he did, the volume of his business experienced a significant increase. At another interim in the meaningful work he was doing, he increased the ratio of his giving even more; again with another leap in both new opportunity and the volume of business activity. After another three increases in the ratio of his giving, he was at the level of giving 95 percent of his profits to Christian work. Toward the end of his life LeTourneau was quoted as saying: "you can't out-give God."

Managing Money and Resources

Moses instructed God's people as a people to not only do what was right, but to LISTEN to the voice of the Lord. In Exodus 15:26 it says: "When you listen carefully to the voice of the Lord your God and do what is right in His eyes, when you pay attention to His direction..." then the people of God as a people would bypass the curses and bondages impacting the world around them. Stewardship in God's economy pivots on this premise.

Two previous chapters addressed the issue of planning with the help of the Holy Spirit. Planning and budgeting are the means to manage and control the use of our finances and resources. In the Appendix is a copy of the Weekly Financial Report we use in our entrepreneurial program.

"Be diligent to know the state of your flocks and attend to your herds." Prov 27: 23

Moreover, as you seek the Lord and mature in listening and obeying His guidance, He will speak "an idea, a concept, an opportunity or wisdom" that will be direction you need to act on. Then, from obeying the voice of the Lord will flow increase.

In Genesis 31 Jacob acted on a dream God gave him. He negotiated wages with Laban based on the sheep (streaked, spotted) that he saw in the dream. The scripture says *"thus Jacob became very prosperous."* After using his boat to teach the people, despite Peter having toiled in that very spot all night, Jesus told Peter to "cast out into the deep." The nets became so full of fish that they began to tear.

Joseph's prophetic gift made room for him. Yet, it was his faithful stewardship while as a slave and prisoner that gained him the reputation that resulted in his promotion. When Joseph was put in charge, he knew what had to be done. While serving Pharaoh, but as God's good steward, he oversaw the largest wealth transfer in the Bible. Joseph went throughout the land of Egypt, coordinating, setting up and preparing for the time of famine.

Bringing Increase to Your Resources

The application of tz'dakah generosity with sound management of resources will serve as the catalyst in bringing increase. The mixture of godly service and attitude enhances the process of bearing fruit.

"In sincerity of heart, fearing the Lord, whatever you do, do it heartily, as to the Lord and not unto men." Colossians 3:22-23

Work. Work is the cornerstone of God's Economy. The passion of one who seeks excellence and enjoys what they do spills-over into producing a long-term customer and community impact. With purposeful work will come growth.

"Let our people learn to maintain good works (fruitful occupations)." Titus 3:14

Cast Vision. Tied to the passion of excellence is the specific purpose the good steward has to be blessed to be a blessing. Key to Joseph's stewardship at each level in his tenure in Egypt was his clear identity in God. From that, Joseph cast vision based on his prophetic gift and his calling. He was God's faithful ambassador at each step.

Creativity and Resourcefulness. The most significant part of entrepreneurship (to identify opportunity and know what to do) will come from God's creative direction and unlimited resources.

"The Lord said to Moses, 'when you go back to Egypt, see that you do all those wonders before Pharaoh which I have put in your hand.'" Exodus 4:21

Enterprise: Buy and Sell. Establishing independence within God's economy by starting a business is the mark of trusting in the Lord and good stewardship. It is a process of building through buying and selling.

"Buy and sell until I return." Luke 19:13

Undervalued Assets. Jesus explained a key dimension of the

Kingdom through the business truth of the one who has the wisdom to recognize and take advantage of undervalued assets. It reflects the priority to be given in response to the level of timely opportunity, when one identifies a true, undervalued asset, such as the undervalued pearl..

"The Kingdom is like a merchant seeking beautiful pearls, who when he found one particular pearl of great value, sold all that he had and bought it." Matthew 13:45-46

Miracles. Miracles are God's provision apart from any other source. When stewardship in bringing increase has faithfully employed every step from work to enterprise; in God's economy there can be the expectation of His periodic supernatural intervention. It cannot be overlooked that Jesus used Peter's gift as a fisherman to provide the miracle he needed for the unexpected tax requirement.

"When Peter needed to pay taxes, Jesus told him: 'Go fishing and the first fish you get, take the gold coin out of its mouth.'" Matthew 17:27

The Authority from Faithful Stewardship

Dominion comes through faithful stewardship over time. It represents an authority and favor that overcomes in the face of the spiritual climate of a world held in the bondage of corruption. It is the means by which we mobilize believers in lands of persecution to operate against overwhelming odds of adversity. It is the Kingdom mandate by which we employ righteous power in overcoming evil with good.

When tz'dakah-level charitable righteousness is combined with a community that listens to the voice of the Lord, what lies ahead will be a pathway primed with supernatural opportunity. This dynamic is punctuated by the story of a unique Russian congregation we imparted our God's economy program to in early 2007.

In a community 800 miles from Moscow, a group of Christians purchased and took possession of the tenth most significant historical site in all of Russia. It is a palace once owned by Lenin. This congregation, birthed in the mid-nineties, is extremely active and has made its mark in its community by serving.

They have made a difference with social programs where government programs have not. Among their outreaches in serving their community has been an effective drug-rehab center, a medical outreach and a prisoner rehab program that have transformed those they ministered to into active, model citizens. Despite the authorities still carrying an anti-Christian bias held from years past, when it came to approval of this congregation's purchase of this former palace, now a community center, the word was that the decision was based on: "give them whatever they want, they're doing so much good." As good stewards, they are paving a pathway of opportunity for the Kingdom, by being blessed to be a blessing.

CHAPTER 8

OPPORTUNITY IN TURBULENT TIMES

"Beware of those who will betray you,
but know this will yield opportunity."
Matthew 10:17-19

Throughout the Word of God, we have a mandate to be blessed to be a blessing. With God as our Senior Partner, in subtle ways that defy the world's way of life, we have become God's opportunity brokers.

"So then, while we have opportunity, let us do good to all men, but especially to those who are of the household of faith." Galatians 6:10

Jesus warned those choosing to follow Him that He was sending us out as sheep among wolves and to be as wise as serpents and as harmless as doves. He went on to admonish us to be wary of those who would betray us, BUT to know that in the midst of adversity and persecution we would find opportunity.

Prophetically, we have entered strange, uncertain and fast-changing times. The serious tempo marking these times calls for something more. However, despite the need to be on our guard against the world's enticements and traps, these are also times of opportunity. They are times bearing a unique significance for both my "Joseph Calling" and "God's economy" messages.

In early 1996 I wrote: "A time is coming soon when there will be changes in the infrastructures of the world's systems that will create reversals resulting in discontinuities such as the world has never seen. In the same manner that Joseph the patriarch was sent ahead to prepare for what was coming to the earth, God is today sending individuals ahead to prepare for a time of great change that will precede the shift of all ages. These will be individuals who clearly hear God's voice and who possess a unique understanding of the times, who will be thrust into positions of influence within the economic, governmental and business infrastructures that guide the course of world events."

From the beginning, God's people have been called to be a light to the world around them. God told Abraham that He would make his name great, that he would be a blessing; and that through him, those who accepted his testimony and blessed him, would in return be mightily blessed. So it was and so it will be for those who bear the Name of the Lord.

Abraham was a good steward. He demonstrated the reality of God to the world around him through an economic community with God at the center. His influence as a man of God changed the spiritual climate around him. He was a community builder who built from the bottom up.

Joseph the Patriarch on the other hand operated uniquely from within the world's system. His stewardship and prophetic gift made room for him. Yet, despite totally different circumstance with adversity arrayed against him, he also demonstrated the reality of God. He stewarded opportunity as a most unlikely candidate, without position, from the bottom-up; to a point to when God intervened and he became a prototype of establishing God's authority and rule from the top-down.

Joseph became a model of harnessing opportunity in turbulent times for God's purposes, while providing a safe haven for both his benefactors and God's people in the process. The dynamic of over-riding the spiritual storm approaching the world at that time carries a parallel to the times before us and the approach needed in the face of adversity.

The Signs of the Times

Jesus strongly admonished those following him to anticipate and respond strategically to the signs of the times.

"When you see a cloud rising in the west, you say, 'A shower is coming'; and so it is. When you see the south wind blow, you say, 'There will be hot weather'; and there is. So, why do you discern the face of the sky and the earth, but not the times?" Luke 12: 54-56

In understanding the times, there's been an economic shift: the rules have changed. The US Airways flight going down into the Hudson River in January of 2009 provides a prophetic snapshot of the economic meltdown preceding this event. Miraculously, it was a soft landing, as was the meltdown. However as a precursor to our entrance into more turbulent times with unexpected crises ahead; not unlike the time in which Joseph interpreted Pharaoh's dream, it marks this as a TIME TO PREPARE (See Chapter 11).

The Bottom-Up, Top-Down Matrix

Over the centuries, God's matrix for opportunity through His people has included both bottom-up and top-down economic approaches. Each demonstrates His reality to the observing world and each brings change to the spiritual climate. Joseph spent many years faithfully as a community-builder before the set-times that resulted in him being handed the top-down mantle.

The calling, as was Joseph's, to the top-down economy will involve alliances with Pharaoh-like gatekeepers during turbulent times; who serve to create the means to bypass disaster and provide refuge and provision for God's people. With 53 of the largest 100 economies in the world being corporations, the potential for modern-day Joseph-Pharaoh alliances no doubt will extend beyond the prospect of nation-states.

The bottom-up calling entails entrepreneurial community builders, business owner administrators who serve their communities and mobilize God's people, keeping them safe.

Cycles of Opportunity

Discerning opportunity begins with understanding the stage of the economic cycle. Just as the Bible (Genesis 8) describes the perpetual cycles in nature, such as seedtime and harvest, so there is a parallel with economic cycles. The Apostle Paul alludes to these cycles as times of abasing and times of abounding.

"I know how to be abased and I know how to abound." Philippians 4:11

Harvest will be a time of reaping and gathering. Everything is in abundance. On the other hand, seedtime is the opposite. It is a time following winter when reserves are low, but with a sufficient amount set aside for the new planting season.

So times of abasing, as described by Paul are times of sowing. They are vulnerable times, more subject to attacks of the enemy. These are times when it is important to be content, to avoid complaining and to maintain tz'dakah generosity.

During times of abundance, it is important to avoid the bottomless pit of materialism and a consumptive lifestyle. These are times to give unique focus to the leading of the Holy Spirit in planning, as consideration is given to future turns in the cycles with prudent diversification. These are times to buy low; to look for undervalued assets. Maintaining generosity, tz'dakah and community responsibility should be an ongoing priority in both the abasing and abundance cycles. However, acting on opportunity requires wisdom on understanding the times and discerning the cycle.

Discerning the Change in the Cycle. When Jesus came walking on the water, the disciples cried out with fear. Jesus said, "It is I; do not be afraid." Only Peter saw the change and the opportunity; and asked the Lord to confirm what he was discerning. The dynamic of Jesus walking on the water was clearly a "new thing." Peter stepping out of the boat and moving toward Jesus on the water was triggered by Peter asking Jesus for a word of confirmation and in receiving it, him acting on it.

When the cycle shifts and change is considered, wisdom begins with determining if we see the Lord in it; and if so, by asking the Lord for a word of confirmation.

In 1977, I began discerning the Lord nudging me toward launching my own business. Without a business background, I was more than a little uncomfortable with this prospect. Yet, as I describe in my *God's Economy, Israel and the Nations* book, the Lord increasingly impressed upon me the importance of my taking this step of faith; and that He would be with me. In retrospect, I had no way of knowing the timing and alignment of the opportunity. The cycle for my entrance into this venture was at its optimum.

At the time, however, all I knew was that without the Lord, my probability of failure was imminent. Nevertheless, I was convinced God was in it; and He indeed was giving me strong confirmation.

So, I risked everything we had to enable this step of obedience. What followed opened the vistas to a journey, an adventure with the Lord that continues to this day. What also followed was the entrance into opportunity that never could have happened within the limitations and constraints of serving as someone else's employee. God was thrusting me into a position of influence and making me the head and not the tail. As I navigated this pathway, the unfolding opportunity released potential that impacted not only the extent of my calling, but my clientele and our employees, my community and the Kingdom. It also began a shift in my awareness of what it meant to be an opportunity enabler.

Mind-Sets for Changing Times

The mind-sets needed for times of change must embrace a trust focused on the Lord and His economy and not on the world's system. That entails the need for specific predispositions in our attitudes and response to several key factors.

Kingdom. Kingdom mind-sets operate with a complete dependency on the Lord and are driven by the merging of the spiritual, economic and community. Kingdom mind-sets are a paradox to the way the world employs power: We live by dying. We lead by serving. We gain by giving. Order comes from change. Wisdom comes from simplicity. In short, success is defined by humility and service.

Entrepreneurial – Increase. An entrepreneurial mind-set creatively paves the way past adversity to identify opportunity and build something of value with a purpose.

Community – Tz'dakah. A community mind-set and focus is one that serves and enables opportunity for others. As Paul admonished the Galatians to do good to all, but with priority given to the believing community; the process results in opportunity multiplying as ripples of blessings go out to the extended communities around us.

Isaiah 58. Isaiah 58 embraces God's heart with consideration given to the poor and needy. It is at the heart of the mind-set of an opportunity-enabler. The promises of God's blessings multiply to those operating with an Isaiah 58 heart.

"If there is a poor man among your brothers, do not be hard-hearted or tight-fisted towards your poor brother. Rather be open-handed and freely lend him whatever he needs. Give generously without a grudging heart; so the LORD will bless you in all the work of your hands." Deuteronomy 15: 7-11

Resource. Monetary values can experience sudden shifts. The thinking needed for changing times recognizes and anticipates the cycles and identifies the resources where tangible value will be maintained.

Hebraic – Israel. The pinnacle of change taking place in the world will be tied to developments in Israel, with the response unveiled in the Jewish roots to the faith.

Refuge Gatekeepers. Discerning modern-day Pharaohs and the opportunity for Kingdom alliances can be expected to carry increased significance in the days ahead.

Differentiating the Opportunity Enablers

At the crux of the Joseph-calling is the function of discerning and acting on opportunity during hard times. It calls for a solid maturity in the Lord, rather than the exploits of the wannabes; the arrogantly ambitious, high rollers and spiritual social climbers who are blind to the cost.

A glimpse of the dynamics of this calling begins by recognizing that Joseph operated in a religiously unorthodox context. Yet it was uniquely what the Lord chose for him. Joseph was totally immersed in the world's system! Despite that, his spiritual identity as God's ambassador was clearly established. This secular alliance that brought fullness to God's purposes was an *interlinking of secular enterprises with overriding Kingdom objectives.*

Today's Josephs are trusted servant-leaders who have a clear call and mandate from the Lord; men and women who God has uniquely prepared and who KNOW HOW TO PREPARE.

These are people who are untouched and unfazed by mammon or the world's power. They are opportunity brokers employing righteous power, whose overwhelming motivation is to serve God's Kingdom. They are people with unusual foresight, who clearly hear God's voice, as well as reflecting a gifting and ability to recognize opportunity and know what to do about it. It is a calling that demands much more than the expectation of being extremely talented.

The pivotal dimension differentiating Joseph from others with unique talents and abilities was something more than his sterling character; it was more than his dream interpretation or his brilliant plan. The words of Pharaoh reveal the differentiating factor: *"Can we find such a one as this, a man in whom is the Spirit of God? In as much as God has shown you all this, there is no one as wise and discerning as you are."* Genesis 41:38

Joseph's promotion was the result of the recognition of the prophetic wisdom operating in Joseph that Pharaoh saw as coming from the Lord.

A few years ago, one of the leaders we have worked with in Asia received a unique prophetic word from a high-level prophet. He seized the opportunity. The timing was such that he would have never acted on his own. From the simple steps of obedience with his involvement with seemingly commonplace ventures has come increase. With the increase have come ripples of impact, as he has served as an opportunity enabler.

The deception operating against many with this calling has been a mind-set constrained by a focus on their own opportunity and the prospect of doing wonderful things "when their ship comes in." This brother, on the other hand, had the maturity and faithfulness to give priority to his efforts as an opportunity enabler as the process establishing him developed. His efforts have ranged from providing scholarships to committed Christian young people, to helping establish funds to launch new entrepreneurs, to community benevolence during natural disasters.

"His lord said to him, 'Well done, good and faithful servant; you were faithful over a few things, I will make you ruler over many things.'" Matthew 25:21

Joseph the patriarch was a faithful steward at each level during his tenure in Egypt: while as a slave in Potiphar's house; then as a man entrusted with authority while a prisoner; all of which set the stage for his promotion and role along side Pharaoh.

Joseph was driven by faith, NOT fear. At each stage, he had a clear understanding of his sphere and his authority in God. At each stage, he identified and maximized opportunity.

The Pathway to Opportunity

During turbulent times, the pathway to opportunity begins with a heightened awareness of the snares that need to be avoided. Difficult times will mar the distinction between viable trends and fads. During great change it will be prudent to avoid premature steps and any type of frenzied need to act or to force issues; to "make something happen." Special care should be given to avoid superficial illusions from the media and pop culture. More than ever, times of change demand quieting our hearts before the Lord and gleaning His guidance with greater clarity.

Times of uncertainty need to give greater discernment to the difference between the supernatural that comes from God and that which amounts to magic and the weird. It also means avoiding the traps of business-as-usual, blind loyalty and the deceptions of conforming to political correctness. Above all, is the need to guard against getting entrapped by chasing money. Deuteronomy 28 emphasizes that: "All these blessings shall come upon us and overtake us when we are listening to the voice of the Lord." Money is not the objective, it's the byproduct.

The point is that the pathway to opportunity during times of discontinuity will be through a genuine Holy Spirit partnership. It will be marked by the mantle of Abraham as we serve as opportunity enablers. Opportunity extended operates as a catalyst to releasing additional opportunity.

The pathway of opportunity is a pathway that taps into power, but not as the world understands power, but with the righteous power that operates through God in community. It is the power described by 1 Peter 2:15 that "By your good works, you'll put to silence the ignorance of foolish men."

It is the power of influence. Not to be confused with clever manipulation, influence builds, brings increase and releases others into the blessings of God. It is the power that operates through simplicity in God's economy; as we produce more with less. It is the power that defines your sphere or boundaries of authority described in 2 Corinthians 10:13: "As their faith grows [those you're enabling], so you will be within your sphere enlarged even more."

Enabling opportunity, while navigating turbulence, is a potent leadership pathway with results that implant God's Kingdom rule. It pivots on making God your Senior Partner and entering the flow of His guidance. It involves an Isaiah 58 heart that extends itself to maximizing your combined gifts and anointing, as you are blessed to be a blessing. It involves paying the cost of acquiring the authority and anointing to match the calling. All of which combine to embracing the distinction of your Kingdom citizenship.

CHAPTER 9

COMMUNITY BUILDING

*"For creation itself longs for the revealing of the sons of God
that it might be delivered from the bondage of corruption
as it gains entrance into this glorious freedom."*
Romans 8:19-21

B iblical community is the pinnacle of God's people operating
together with a common purpose. Abraham portrayed the model
with the interrelated dimensions of being God-centered, entrepreneurial and community-driven. The Jewish Torah (Pentateuch) gives
keen focus to the operating principles for biblical community. Jesus
indicated when the community of God's people function together as
God intends that it demonstrates God's reality and draws the world
to Himself.

*"Let your light shine before men that they may see your good works,
and glorify your Father who is in heaven."* Matthew 5:16

While the world has come up with many approaches to community; none begin to compare. Biblical community is an expression
of both the discipline and maturity of its members. It thrives on a
high-level of trust and service, fueled by the community dynamic
of tz'dakah, which is charitable righteousness. It grows through
a unique use of spiritual power driven by servant leadership. It is
a safe place of spiritual nurturing, while simultaneously being an

incubator for the encouragement and growth of the giftings of its members. With that will be a common higher purpose that endures beyond its generations.

According to the standards in the Jewish Mishnah, the smallest element of community is known as a minyan. Whenever ten Jews live within walking distance of one another, a minyan is formed. This small group serves simultaneously as the most basic element for public worship; but also as a means of mutual support and connection in order to cultivate the success of its members.

Then, when a hundred Jews are within walking distance, they form a congregation, which continues to serve the same functions on a larger scale. These proactive approaches to community address the realities of a people of faith living in a corrupt world. It's the basis of Jesus' charge to be a light to the world.

God's Gift of Community

The biblical response to the oppression, affliction and sorrow evident in the world's system is tz'dakah or righteous charity, which is community faith-in-action. However, far more proactive than benevolence, Jewish tradition holds that the highest form of tz'dakah is helping someone to start a small business. This community standard within Judaism upholds that none within the community will go hungry or be homeless. Members of the community take care of their own.

As such, community is a gift of God, the unique elements of which are unveiled in Psalm 107. This psalm describes the reality of the challenge of living in a fallen world; and the solution that keeps God's people from being seduced and overcome by the evil that devours and evolves into the stronghold called wickedness.

Community. Biblical community is a safe place with God at the center. In the opening verses of this psalm, when God's people reach out to Him, the foundational step in this divine protection and provision is in establishing community.

"They wandered in the wilderness in a desolate way; they found no city [community; safe place] to dwell in. Hungry and thirsty,

their soul fainted in them. Then they cried out to the LORD in their trouble, and He delivered them out of their distresses. He led them forth by the right way, that they might find a city [community] for a dwelling." Psalm 107:4-7

Righteousness. The second step in the development of biblical community is breaking the bondages of corruption and establishing the biblical standard of community righteousness.

"They sat in darkness and in the shadow of death, bound in afflic-tion and irons; because they rebelled against the Words of God, and despised the counsel of the Most High. Then they cried out to the LORD in their trouble. He brought them out of darkness and the shadow of death, and broke their chains in pieces." Psalm 107:10-14

Spiritual Autonomy. As the community matures, previously subtle, but embedded evil will manifest giving challenge to the spiritual authority within the community. The result of this community dis-harmony releases afflictions that either needs to be cleansed or removed. When that takes place, God's supernatural power will be released.

"Fools, because of their transgression, and because of their iniqui-ties, were afflicted. Their soul abhorred all manner of food, and they drew near to the gates of death. Then they cried out to the LORD in their trouble. He sent His Word and healed them, and delivered them from their destructions." Psalm 107:17-20

Dominion. When the community has developed to the stage of embracing its common purpose, there will be challenges that need to be overcome in making it self-sufficient and a means to facilitate increase and provision for its members. Establishing God's authority over the resisting elements is foundational to God's original purpose for creating man: to rule over the work of His hands. It involves a proactive community response to their dependency on God.

"Those who go down to the sea in ships, who do business on great waters, they see the works of the LORD, and His wonders in the deep. They mount up to the heavens, they go down again to the depths; their soul melts because of trouble. They reel to and fro, and stagger like a drunken man, and are at their wits' end. Then they cry out to the LORD in their trouble. He calms the storm, so that its waves are still. Then they are glad because they are quiet; so He guides them to their desired haven." Psalm 107:23-30

This incredibly revealing Psalm goes on to give a picture of the conflict going on in the world. It explains the consequences to corrupt power; and the eventual righteous intervention of the Lord when oppression, affliction and sorrow amass in manifesting against the righteous.

God-Centered Community

The dynamic of God-centered community evolves around a shared identity. With the foundation of this shared identity in God will be a unity that comes from a common purpose that brings increase and provision; and serves to the benefit and development of the entire community.

Tz'dakah extends opportunity to all. It impacts the way that "increase" is handled. Contrary to the way the world normally operates, the Torah admonishes us not to squeeze everything we can out of a deal. In the Jewish principle known to this day as gleaning, room should be given for part of the increase to spill over to the poor and less fortunate; allowing them the dignity of work in order to establish themselves.

"When you are harvesting in your field and overlook a sheaf, do not go back to get it. Leave it for the foreigner, the fatherless and the widow, so that the Lord your God may bless you in all the work of your hands. When you beat the olives from your trees, do not go over the branches a second time. When you harvest the grapes in your vineyard, do not go over the vines again. Leave what remains for the foreigner, the fatherless and the widow." Deuteronomy 24:19-21

Having served the leadership of communities of believers in nineteen nations, I've seen an array of communities-in-action. These range from the most common conception of a community of believers: as the regular attendees of Sunday services; to the more proactive members of the persecuted Body who encourage opportunity for its members and are a true light to the extended community around them.

One of the more dynamic groups we have extended our program to is a Messianic congregation in the Former Soviet Union. Its members participate, as one, in an Alpha Course specially adapted to engage the Jewish community spiritually. They have a special approach to honoring and serving holocaust survivors. They are responsive to the needs of those in lack.

However, one of their more dynamic initiatives is their entrepreneurial groups that we helped them set up. Based on the minyan concept, these groups are led by spiritually mature persons with business ownership expertise, who meet twice a month. These two hour sessions include the first hour for prayer requests directed toward the success of existing businesses; or for the businesses being planned. The second hour is an interactive time of sharing wisdom designed to develop plans, overcome hurdles and otherwise foster the success of its members. In short, these minyan-sized groups build community by serving the dual purpose of spiritual mentoring and business incubators for people of faith. They'll be explained in more detail in the next chapter.

Community Builders

In his letter to the Ephesians, Paul clearly explains the key elements in this dynamic for building biblical community. Nurturing and harnessing the combined gifts of its members serves the common purpose of a higher good for the community and the Kingdom.

"For because of Him the whole body, closely joined and firmly knit together by the joints and ligaments with which it is supplied, when each part [with power adapted to its need] is working properly [in all its functions], grows to full maturity, building itself up in love." Ephesians 4:16 (AMP)

When God-centered community develops according to this standard there will come a maturity in the way it operates, that not only releases its members into their callings, but prepares them with a mantle of leadership, each within their own sphere.

It is the "something more" spiritual dimension that can only be ascribed to working together in unity under the power of His Spirit. It is released to the members who become enablers; who facilitate opportunity for others. This enablement of opportunity is at the core of those we describe as community builders.

Job was a genuine community-builder. God was preparing him for promotion; for something more that only could have come from God. His friends misread the intent of his reversals with their limited view of success. Job not only prevailed, but despite the dubious part played by his friends, was instrumental through his prayers in bringing them with him, as he was released into new, higher dimensions in his effectual role as a community builder.

Community builders advance God-centeredness. They exhibit tz'dakah in all their endeavors. Community builders embrace community responsibility and provide an entrepreneurial, growth orientation with their activities. They are people who demonstrate integrity, fairness and trust in all they do; while promoting the work ethic. Community builders operate with faith as risk-takers and cultivate both vision and opportunity among other members of the community.

The bottom line is that community building is the practical application of the exponential of man ruling over the work of God's hands. Community builders serve as enablers and replicate themselves. They mobilize and enrich the function of others to serve in building community with the balance between the spiritual and economic riches of His glory. They are catalysts for growth among gatherings of those breaking the mold and embracing the model of God-centered entrepreneurial community. Community builders are leaders and examples in their own entrepreneurial community building agendas. They are standard-bearers for the model, the mandate and mantle; as servant-leaders advancing the community good.

The Community Builder Challenge

The community builder challenge is in bringing change and making a difference through community. At its core is the mobilization and equipping of the believing entrepreneurial community; the nurturing of the combined gifts; the impartation of a Kingdom perspective; the release of the entrepreneurial initiative; and opening the gates for their light to shine while building bridges with the broader community.

In the next chapter we will address the dynamics of the strategy we use to build community builders; how in environments hostile to people of faith, to make God's people to be the head and not the tail.

SECTION IV:

LEADERSHIP FOR CHANGE

CHAPTER 10

STRATEGY FOR CHANGE

"I told them of the hand of God strong upon me, and of the king's words. So they said, let us rise up and build. So they set their hands to do this good work."
Nehemiah 2:18

B iblical community is God's catalyst for change in a fallen world. At the same time, it is designed as a self-sustaining, safe harbor. It grows by replication and service. Its foundational challenge is one of leadership: in mobilizing and equipping its members to operate with the mandate, model and mantle that God intends for his people (See Chapter 1).

Moses' father-in-law Jethro advised Moses to select capable people with upright hearts and then begin reproducing in them his role as a leader, both for his good and for the good of the community. This wisdom is at the heart of the goal of community leadership, which is to build community builders.

"Teach them the principles and precepts; then show them the path in which they must walk; then give them the work that they must do."
Exodus 18: 20

The issue begs the question of why? Why is God-centered community so vital to righteous power being employed in a corrupt world? The simple answer is that before you can disciple nations

(Matt 28), you need the maturity and visible impact from discipling community. It's the wisdom behind Jesus telling us that we would be the light of the world; a city [community] set on a hill that cannot be hidden (Matt 5:14).

Being the light of the world demands cultural leadership. Regardless of the locale, the culture MUST be a Kingdom culture in order to carry the visibility and influence of God-centered community to the world around it. The point of demarcation is defined by the community identity being in God. When the community identity in God is weak or watered-down, the Light is diffused and defiled. On the other hand, when the Light is pure, even as the dark gets darker, it will shine more brightly. Two-thirds of the world lives under already tough spiritual environments. The majority of what remains is at risk with evil systematically creeping into the infrastructures.

Community Leadership

Over the ages, it has been the simple things, employed by God's people that have brought results exceeding expectations. These simple things have confounded the wise. They pivot on hearing and obeying the voice of the Lord, with the distinctive of a God-centered identity. It operates with stewarding a mantle of a people flowing in oneness with God; a mantle passed down from generation to generation (Deut 11:19). When these factors, based on God's Word, converge in their community application, they become the foundation for those known by His Name becoming the head and not the tail; operating as a society of leaders.

"The one who sits on the throne as king must copy these Words in a book. He must always keep a copy of this Word with him and read it daily as long as he lives. This regular reading of God's Word will prevent him from becoming proud and acting as if he is above his fellow people. It will also prevent him from falling away from God's Word in the smallest way." Deuteronomy 17:18-20 NLT

In the previous chapter I gave an example of minyan-sized groups that fuel the self-sustaining life of the community. These groups, which operate within congregations, meet regularly for the purpose of growing spiritually as entrepreneurial ambassadors; as community builders. Their potential has been proven in spiritually challenging arenas, ranging from the Former Soviet Union to Asia where we have set this biblical community development dynamic in motion.

It is based on a program of spiritual mentorship that serves to birth small business enterprises and to build community-builders. It nurtures this community phenomenon and spawns leaders; opportunity enablers who advance the God-centered entrepreneurial initiative and releases destiny for individuals, as well as for the community. It's the foundation to discipling community.

"The things which you have heard from me in the presence of many witnesses, entrust these to faithful men who will be able to teach others also." 2 Timothy 2:2

It incorporates the elements reviewed in the last several chapters that unlock the destiny of community builders. These elements include:

- Planning
- Hearing God's Voice
- Defining and Releasing the Gifts
- Nurturing the Entrepreneurial
- Stewardship
- Enabling Opportunity
- Building Community

The Process for Community Change
The bottom line is in creating the seedbed to bring purposeful change; to make a difference, enabling opportunity by entering the arena God has outlined for those known by His Name to become the head and not the tail. It involves releasing business destiny; opportunity discovery and the means of increase for the community good.

The process includes twice monthly gatherings of entrepreneurs and potential entrepreneurs. These local groups should be set up to enable ease of attendance for all its members. They typically can range in size from a half dozen to fifteen. They are led by persons who are spiritually mature whose experience includes some form of business ownership. Each gathering is two hours, which serves specifically the purpose of directed prayer for the business goals of its members; and as a means to seek God, share wisdom and nurture both the success and God-purpose represented by each business. The members hold each other accountable.

During the first hour, the leader of the group will distribute prayer requests which each member has prepared beforehand. These prayer requests are specific to their business or their plans for starting a business and reflect four or five one-line descriptions of operational needs for their enterprise. The group then prays for these practical needs and goals.

The potency of the prayer of small gatherings that meet regularly should never be underestimated. Jesus said where two or more are gathered in His Name, there He would be (Matthew 18:20).

Several years ago, I assumed an executive position in an organization with 423 employees. Despite a strong population of Christians in this organization, the impact of a local witchcraft coven, whose members were also represented, had resulted in the Christians largely in cautious hiding. I used my position to start two different prayer groups. The prayer groups then multiplied and over time changed the spiritual climate of the organization. The fervency of small, informal gatherings has literally changed the spiritual climate in nations around the world.

The second hour will be interactive among the members, led by the wisdom of its leader(s). It represents a 2 Timothy 2:2 mentoring approach, whereby each member develops, refines, prays for and sets in motion planning goals that bear on their business destiny. These planning goals give shape to the mix of the individual's gifts and calling, along with the opportunity and goals with those that their skills or talents will serve and with that, the means by which God will be glorified by the impact of their enterprise on the broader community.

These planning goals include: the natural gifts, the spiritual gifts, those being served, the dream in serving others, gateways of opportunity, mentors, vision as a community builder, long-term goals, and strategies for the common good.

The Natural Gifts. A person's natural gift is something they flow in naturally. When developed sufficiently, it becomes an exceptional talent and the basis to be commercialized. The process of mentoring gives special focus and discernment to identifying and fostering this key factor underlying one's calling and destiny in God.

The Spiritual Gifts. There are different levels of spiritual gifts. However, the seven motivational gifts described in Romans 12 (exhorter, mercy, giving, serving, leadership, prophetic, teacher) are fundamental. A person's primary (strongest) motivational gift represents the value-added and power behind the way their natural gift flows most spontaneously. In the appendix is a succinct description of how each of the Romans 12 gifts operates.

Those Being Served. Understanding the particular needs of those served and who they are in terms of their unique characteristics is vital to being able to reach them with a service that provides something of value in terms of meeting these needs.

The Dream in Serving Others. When the natural and spiritual gifts are operating together, they represent a potent means of serving others. Being able to describe the "destiny dream," in their application of serving others, is vital to mapping out a pathway to making it happen.

Vision as a Community Builder. Tied to the dream of serving others is the vital factor of the vision as a community builder. There should be clarity in what the vision in applying one's gifts to building community is expected to look like when it arrives at maturity. Likewise, it needs to incorporate demonstrated interim steps.

Gateways of Opportunity. At each stage in planning out one's destiny there will be key gateways of opportunity. Sometimes one gateway will open the door to another. However, it is essential to be able to understand and know how to realistically penetrate these gateways of opportunity.

Mentors. Everyone needs two or three mentors, persons who have a track record and are seasoned experts in the area of a person's calling. A mentor is much more than someone with an opinion; but rather a trust relationship with the specific wisdom that can be brought to the plate from building something of similar value in their own sphere.

Long-Term Goals. The purpose of the interaction in these support groups is to keep the vision alive, while dealing with operational and spiritual realities that emerge along the way. Maintaining viable goals with a grasp of expectations in a five year time-frame is essential to this process.

Strategies for the Community Good. Developing strategies to accomplish the goals on a long term basis is essential to grasping the realities needed to give shape to the short-term operational steps targeted in the first hour of the gathering. These longer-term strategies merge the practical means of accomplishing enterprise growth while progressively being blessed to be a blessing to customers and the community.

Defining and refining each of these factors will change over time as they are developed. Planning is a process. Any enterprise worth its salt will evolve, as it becomes a means of influence to those within its sphere. Opportunity will manifest from timing factors and the shape that an enterprise takes as it grows.

As the twice monthly gatherings seek God, share their wisdom and nurture both the spiritual purpose and success of the businesses of its members; its members will grow. As the group grows, leaders will be identified who are then groomed through responsibility in assistant leadership positions. As new leaders are developed and ascend into full leadership, the more experienced leaders take on new members to mentor and create new groups.

"As their faith grows, so you will be within your sphere enlarged even more." 2 Corinthians 10:15

Within the community, these small groups will profit from quarterly gatherings to share wisdom, testimonies and fellowship. The bottom line is that the spiritual mentoring of business destiny through prayer and the interactive employment of the "destiny planning" elements will build the community.

The Challenge of Kingdom Change

Kingdom change begins with our stewardship of community. The proactive employment of minyan-sized groups gives depth to community growth. This simple interaction of group members brings the anointing and clarity to the destinies of its members. The subsequent sowing of the gifts, with purpose, yields enlargement.

This unique community-directed strategy for change will demonstrate the reality of God. By demonstrated good works, it puts to silence the ignorance of foolish men (1 Peter 2:15). In the midst of times of turbulence, it represents a safe place that will turn crisis and corruption into opportunity through God.

Like Joseph the Patriarch, the result will operate against the odds for those willing to pay the cost; of hearing from God and obeying. The distinctive is in a God-centered identity and stewarding "the mantle;" the mantle of the "something more," of being blessed to be a blessing that the world lacks.

This challenge carries a wakeup call and admonishment to begin employing righteous power in a corrupt world as we let our light shine. It requires looking beyond the diminished view of reality held by people around the world, becoming described by far too many as a Western worldview. In a world of superficialities, it addresses the real issues with the transforming model of God-centered entrepreneurial community.

The release of God-centered entrepreneurial community is a program of enlargement and blessing that will change the world. It enables ordinary people to do the extraordinary. At its core is the prophetic dimension of hearing God's voice and making Him your Senior Partner; then mentoring the destiny of those called by His Name. It strengthens its members to become the head and not the tail as the observing world is exposed to the reality of God in operation, through a society of leaders.

"You are the light of the world. A city [community] set on a hill cannot be hidden." Matthew 5:14

CHAPTER 11

PREPARED TO PREPARE

"Justice is turned back and righteousness stands afar off;
for truth is fallen in the street and equity cannot enter. So truth
fails and he who departs from evil makes himself a prey. But the
LORD saw it and it displeased Him. He wondered that there was
no intercessor. According to their deeds He will repay fury to
His adversaries, recompense to His enemies. So when
the enemy comes in like a flood, the Spirit of the LORD
will lift up a standard against him."
Isaiah 59:14-19

We have entered challenging times. It is a time requiring more than what the best of human effort can achieve. With it has been a pathway of preparation into a time of greater purpose; a time of preparation for ones who bear a mantle like Joseph to prepare. The preparation to prepare involves walking through a fire, not unlike what Job, Joseph, Daniel and many other heroes of faith went through.

The Realities of the Times

Religious freedoms that have been taken for granted since the fall of the Iron and Bamboo Curtains are being challenged. There likewise is a struggle underway for the soul of Africa, where on one continent are found the resources sought by the rest of the world.

The spiritual realities taking place in the world today; the creeping, reemerging evil ultimately will affect the entire Body and should provide a sobering perspective that tempers our priorities. The times have experienced a shift and it is time to prepare.

The Fire of Preparation

The story of Job's path through the fire unveils truths pertinent to the righteous being prepared.

Job was a righteous man in the sight of God. He was a spiritual forerunner and business leader of his day. As with Job, the evil one's encounters with today's righteous face a barrier of protection represented by the anointing of God's presence. The barrier was there to enhance God's plans for something more.

Not surprisingly, Satan found access to counter this divine protection. It was through the blindness of ones Job regarded as friends. Contemporaneously, the evil one has employed gateways through the soulish nature of those closest to those being prepared to prepare.

These are inside affiliations the devil can easily provoke with his undermining objectives. These are relationships reflecting a spiritual blindness marked by uncontrolled, spiteful or simply misguided tongues that the enemy can harness to serve his diversionary and destructive tactics.

To accomplish the purposes God had for Job, there was a spiritual level Job had to penetrate. It was a level that superseded his position in the community, his wealth and even his family. It was a spiritual veil leading to a far more mature and richer revelation of not just the Lord, but of Job's high calling. Its pathway involved a fire of preparation.

The Blindness of Job's Friends

Job's friends didn't understand what God was doing in his situation. In their ignorance they spoke of God without true understanding and aligned themselves with the accuser in their conjectures concerning his terrible circumstance. In so doing, they all but pushed Job over the edge. Even before his "friends" showed up, Job's wife had already failed in her role by concluding that Job's only recourse in the face of the onslaught against him was to "curse God and die."

The accusing spirit seeks to find flaws and ultimately destroy.

The accusing spirit operates through soulish seedbeds that take root with idle words; words that have an element of truth with the wrong conclusions; words of judgment without the maturity or authority to judge. Job's accusers added to the pain of the fire he walked through. Some might conclude that it well may have been wagging tongues that precipitated Satan's appeal and access to sift Job in the first place.

Scripture tells us that "life and death are in the power of the tongue" (Proverbs 18:21). James 3 points out that the tongue can be a fire, ignited by hell. So James, speaking to believers, ties tongues of fire to uncontrolled wickedness within the soul, which has a contaminating, depraving and blinding impact on the whole body.

Soulish seedbeds from among "friends" provide the soil for seeds of accusations to take root. Beware of the charmers. Beware of associations marked with issues and hidden agendas, and a track record of providing "inside information" about those operating under the protection of the anointing of God's presence. Beware of the charmers planting accusing seeds that line up with the enemy's intentions to create distraction, division, undermining, and destruction, against the truly righteous.

Evil words have an impact the devil is only too happy to capitalize on. It is the reason Jesus admonished that we will have to give account for every idle word. It is the reason we must look beyond and reach beyond our peripheral cultural vision and give heed to standing in the gap for those outside our spheres of cultural reality, who are undergoing the fire of preparation.

Discerning Evil Intentions

2 Kings 5:25-27 (Amplified Bible) tells the story of how Elisha discerned the evil intentions of his servant Gehazi, who sought to profit from his master's gift by manipulating Naaman, the Syrian. It indicates that Elisha, by the Spirit of God, discerned Gehazi's actions and words. "Elisha said, where have you been, Gehazi? He said, your servant went nowhere. Elisha said to him, did not my spirit go with you when the man turned from his chariot to meet you? Was it a time to accept money, garments, olive orchards, vineyards, sheep, oxen, menservants, and maidservants? Therefore the

leprosy of Naaman shall cleave to you and to your offspring forever. And Gehazi went from his presence a leper as white as snow."

2 Kings 6:10-12 (Amplified Bible) illustrates another dimension tied to the spiritual dynamic of words spoken with evil-intent. It is the story of Elisha's role in spiritually discerning conversations and evil plans the king of Syria had against Israel. "Then the king of Israel sent to the place of which Elisha told and warned him; and thus he protected and saved himself there repeatedly. Therefore the mind of the king of Syria was greatly troubled by this thing. He called his servants and said, will you show me who of us is for the king of Israel? One of his servants said, none, my lord O king; but Elisha, the prophet who is in Israel, tells the king of Israel the words that you speak in your bedchamber."

Evil words spoken in secret will be spiritually discerned and uncovered.

Many years ago while in prayer, a couple I knew repeatedly kept coming to mind. Each time this happened there was a heaviness and sense of darkness as they entered my thoughts. Plus there was an intrusive way in which the thought of them was invading my prayers. It was not at all like the times the Lord would bring someone to mind to pray for. Finally, I just asked the Lord what was happening and why they were coming to mind in this way.

The Lord very clearly answered my inquiry by saying: "They're talking about you, in a negative way." My initial thought was that my own mind was playing tricks on me, and that I didn't need to be giving heed to thoughts of paranoia. However, just in case this response was indeed the Lord, I asked Him to confirm this "word" with a scripture. Less than a half-hour later I was reading the Word and came across the following scripture in Ecclesiastes.

"Curse not the king, no, not even in your thoughts, and curse not the rich in your bedchamber, for a bird of the air will carry the voice, and a winged creature will tell the matter." (Eccl 10:20 Amplified Bible)

What this principle in Ecclesiastes points out is that backbiting and gossip and negative words have an impact on those they target. In effect they are as curses.

Idle and Evil Words of Insiders

Insiders can play a very damaging role in the release of idle, accusing and evil words. This is illustrated in Psalm 55, 12-14 (Amplified Bible): "For it is not an enemy who reproaches and taunts me—then I might bear it; nor is it one who has hated me who insolently vaunts himself against me—then I might hide from him. But it was you, a man my equal, my companion and my familiar friend. We had sweet fellowship together and used to walk to the house of God in company."

Undisciplined, soulishly-driven tongues point to a lack or misuse of leadership and authority. They are signs of spiritual immaturity and unpreparedness. They weaken the unity that God intends within the protective boundaries of community. When the authority of community is undermined, the intentions of evil began infiltrating. The protection of community pivots on the preparedness of its leadership.

The Word comments on the prophet Samuel that: "the Lord let none of his words fall to the ground." This is the way it should be among God's anointed. The words of those anointed for leadership have potency.

When righteous leaders are undermined, it not only removes the protective barriers tied to the leader's authority, but opens the gates for judgment. For Job, the fire was fueled by his wife and then by his friends. When the accuser operates, it seldom is on a single level. It begins with whispers landing at the doorstep of those in close relationship with the one targeted. It can then escalate to levels of judgmental pronouncements unleashing fires of affliction and disarray creating imploding consequences on the entire community.

Job's Friends

It wasn't Job's enemies who came to him during the height of his distress. It was not a committee of distant acquaintances. The scriptures tell us, it was his friends. It was people he trusted; people he should have been able to turn to in tough times.

Job's friends operated behind a thin veil constrained by immaturity, spiritual blindness and wrong priorities. They were predisposed to respond with criticism, complaints and judgment. As community leaders, they projected their limited views, presuming on God and fell short. They saw faults rather than potential. They undermined rather than affirmed. They projected evil rather than protecting.

The words of Job's friends, like those of Job's wife, became fuel for the flames of fire in the hell Job was walking through. Job's friends attempted to deal with spiritual matters judgmentally according to the precepts of men, rather than from God's big-picture perspective (John 7: 18). Job was being prepared. He was a leader of leaders and his authority would bear spiritual impact on the future of the community, as well as generations to come.

God was not happy with Job's friends. The scripture says that His wrath was aroused against them, because they had not spoken of Him what was right, as Job had (Job 42:7-8). It took Job praying for the misfires of his friends; to release them from the judgment they themselves had pronounced, which now stood at their door.

The Gatekeeper Leader Standard: Righteous Power in a Corrupt World

King Saul also dug himself into a hole. His downfall was his concern tied to the words of those he was called to lead. There's a vast difference between being a people-person and one with an emptiness of soul that seeks for the approval of men. It's a distinguishing crux of leadership. Saul lost his calling and destiny because of this heart issue: the fear of man (Proverbs 29:25). His leadership crumbled because of a lack of trust in God; he was obsessed and swayed by what others said and thought.

At the heart of Kingdom leadership is the employment of righteous power in a corrupt world. Saul, like Job served a function of building up, protecting and taking those around him to the next level. Yet, his lack of spiritual maturity, faith and right priorities resulted in him becoming like everyone else and he failed. Kingdom leadership requires something more.

The opening scripture (Isaiah 59:14-19) captures today's setting. Kingdom community-level leaders must be prepared to enter a time of preparing. Facing an onslaught of evil requires an upgrade for the gatekeeper leader who in turn will lift the standard for the community. Job was being prepared in the role as the righteous intercessor-leader sought in Isaiah 59:16. Joseph likewise epitomized that role within a worldly setting. He harnessed the resources of Egypt for God's purposes, while bestowing untold blessings of God on Egypt in the process.

Job repented for his short-sighted, constrained perspective in his role as a righteous (tz'dak) community leader. He weathered the brutal assault of judgment arrayed against him. He repented for limiting God. However, it was when Job prayed for his friends, that his role as gatekeeper-intercessor came to the forefront and his own full release of blessings began.

When Jesus admonished His followers to bless those who curse them, it marked the responsibility of community leaders who serve as gatekeeper-intercessors who stand in the gap on behalf of the community against the incursion of evil and its impending judgment. Job blessed those who had cursed him. That act resulted in him entering into a whole new arena in his role as a leader. It took him into a much higher level of trust in the Lord, with a service to others that was beyond him. Job was a righteous man who became an honorable man.

Honor: The Catalyst to Prepare

Honor kicks in when righteousness becomes devoid of self-righteousness and pride. The story of Job tracks the progression of this attribute of honor.

In Job 29, in defending himself to his friends, Job spoke of how his own honor, glory and strength had previously been constantly renewed: within him. In Job 30, he confessed that with all the terrors being turned upon him, his honor, reputation and welfare had been "chased away."

However, in Job 40, as Job again tried to defend himself along these lines, the Lord challenged Job: to even try, to clothe himself with the honor that only God retains. In the 41st chapter (in the Amplified Bible), something significant happened in Job.

That glimmer of revelation transformed Job's entire perspective in his knowledge of and relationship to the Lord—- and in his own identity, as he acknowledged: "Therefore I now see I have rashly uttered what I did not understand, things too wonderful for me, which I did not know. I had heard of You only by the hearing of the ear, but now my spiritual eye sees You. Therefore I loathe my words and abhor myself and repent in dust and ashes."

The one with honor has no need to be right, but will always support what is right. Real honor is uniquely tied to a righteous heart, one emptied of self and pride and personal agendas and ambitions. It is a heart that has entered into the rest of God spoken of in Hebrews.

The heart at rest is a heart that has ceased from striving and has entered into that level of oneness and harmony with the Lord that we describe as "flowing in His Spirit." Real honor involves a heart that is not hesitant to say it has been wrong. It involves a humble yet generous and magnanimous spirit. An honorable person esteems others higher than themselves. True Kingdom leaders are marked by persons who seek not for promotion or recognition, but service.

While the scripture says that the Lord told Satan that Job was righteous, the subsequent shaking he went through produced an entire new level of righteousness. This subtle truth underscores why judgment first comes to the household of faith. When Job entered into his trials his honor was based on his reputation. However, Job's wife and his friends found flaws and became critics of his reputation. They unconsciously aligned themselves with the designs of the accuser, which was to destroy Job. But the Lord wouldn't allow for Job's destruction.

Honor Bestowed by God. Instead when Job emerged, he possessed an honor and authority bestowed upon him by the Lord. With that was a new identity. The future of Job's accusers wound up at his mercy. Job's transition was from one who was an unqualified righteous man, to one who had become a truly honorable man.

Biblically, to be "honorable" incorporates a righteous heart and wisdom that is always seeking for the higher good. The person who is honorable is one who has a reputation that can be trusted. They can be trusted to be as Nathaniel, one without guile or intrigue; to operate free of hidden agendas and issues. When Jesus prophesied that Nathaniel would see the heavens open and the angels ascending and descending on the Son of man (John 1:51), He was indicating Nathaniel was a man who could be trusted with the secret issues of God's heart.

128

An honorable person is a totally dependable person; one who does not compromise or self-righteously betray. An honorable person is quick to bestow honor, where honor is due. However, a person cannot assume honor or seek for it. It comes from a consistently righteous, humble and unassuming life, one that ultimately is recognized in its wisdom and service to others.

Proverbs has a lot to say about honor. In both the 15th and 18th chapters it says that honor is preceded by humility. Proverbs also says that an honorable man keeps himself far from strife, while a fool is quick to quarrel. Proverbs 21 indicates that the one who earnestly seeks after righteousness, mercy, and loving-kindness will find life, in addition to righteousness and honor. Proverbs also reveals that: *"The reward of humility and the reverent and worshipful fear of the Lord is riches and honor and life."* It also states that pride and honor are incompatible and that: "he who is of a humble spirit will obtain honor." Wisdom and honor work together. Ecclesiastes 10 points out the eroding factor in folly: that even a "little folly in one who is valued for his wisdom will outweigh his wisdom and honor."

Psalm 15 outlines the elements of one walking in honor. The honorable one is one: "….who walks with integrity and works righteousness; and speaks truth in his heart. Who does not slander with his tongue nor does evil to his neighbor, nor takes up a reproach against his friend. In whose eyes a reprobate is despised, but who honors those who fear the Lord. Who swears to his own hurt and does not change. Who does not put out his money at interest, nor take up a bribe against the innocent. He who does these things will never be shaken."

True honor begets an unusual level of authority. It is an authority that is laced with humility and the fear of the Lord: the type of authority evidenced in Joseph, even while he was still a slave and in prison. True honor is a catalyst for a high level of faith. True honor within a community leader is a magnet for the wisdom of God and carries a mandate to prepare.

Maturity and Leadership: The Gateway to Prepare

We have entered a time in which a creeping evil is penetrating the world we live in. It is an evil seeking entrance and infiltration into righteous circles of influence within both the world and the Body. It is an evil targeting God's very elect. Yet over the centuries, God has had Jobs, Josephs, Daniels and other leaders of honor who would face and overcome the inroads of evil for the good of God's people.

Kingdom leaders serve first as gatekeeper-intercessors. They wield the maturity, trust and authority to stand in the gap, at the gate so to speak, on behalf of the community for which they are responsible. With that function is the role to prepare. Kingdom leaders bear the responsibility to raise the standard for the community, as the community serves an inward role of protection and an outward role as a light to the world around them. They raise the standard of community maturity. In so doing, they create safe havens against the inroads of evil.

With the gatekeeper-intercessor's pushback against evil will come the purifying fire that results in a shift in the foundations from which the Body operates. It is a shift brought to the forefront through those prepared for pivotal times: those prepared with the maturity and authority to face the fires and to prepare. These are ones who have been willing to pay the cost of the fire; which like Job, may involve their position in the community, their wealth and even their family.

These are ones called by God to penetrate the fabric of society with God's initiatives and focus. These are men and women of God, untainted and sold-out as Joseph the Patriarch was when he emerged as God's man of honor for the hour, when he was promoted to sit alongside of Pharaoh and entrusted with the mantle to prepare.

These are anointed ones, like Job, who have persevered and penetrated that constraining spiritual barrier, who are emerging from the fire without the smell of smoke.

For those emerging from this time of preparation, it will involve much greater responsibilities: for their communities, nations and resources. It will involve unique pathways by which the Kingdom is advanced, not by the approval or precepts of men, but rather the employment of righteous power in corrupt settings that brings the change that delivers from the bondage of corruption; the change that demonstrates the reality of God in the context of worldly settings.

The days have become evil. Yet, God's power is not only greater, but His anticipatory strategies will mark this as a time of incredible opportunity for those He has found trustworthy to prepare, in the midst of reversals and discontinuities.

"Have you entered the treasury of snow, or have you seen the store-house of hail, which I have reserved for the time of trouble, for the day of battle and war?"

"The LORD has opened His armory, and has brought out the weapons of His indignation; for this is the work of the Lord God of hosts." Job 38: 22, 23 and Jeremiah 50:25

CHAPTER 12

SOCIETY OF LEADERS

*"Arise, shine, for your light has come and the glory of the
Lord has arisen upon you. For darkness shall cover the earth
and deep darkness the peoples. But the Lord has arisen over you
and His glory will be seen upon you. Gentiles shall come to
your light and kings to the brightness of your rising."*
Isaiah 60:1-3

These are extraordinary times. They are times when knowing-what-to-do takes something more.

Mounting turbulence in global affairs shouts that it no longer is business as usual. America is divided. China is pursuing economic dominance. Russia seems intent on regaining its role as bully. Iran is plowing a nuclear pathway. Israel has been targeted for annihilation. International economies are being blind-sided with short term fixes. Globally, beguiling policies mask realities. Terrorism is a global threat and lawlessness abounds. In all this, more than two thirds of the world's population lives under what the Psalmist calls oppression, affliction and sorrow.

The issue is one of power, as the time-clock hastens toward the power shift of all ages, described by Isaiah.

*"The abundance of the sea will be turned to you. The wealth of the
nations will come to you."* Isaiah 60:5

In the midst of the churning, God has a plan and a strategy. It involves a dimension of "something more" than the best of what the world has to offer.

This something more has historical precedent with the biblical heroes of faith. Joseph the Patriarch demonstrated it under the most adverse of circumstances. Daniel exercised it when immersed in a culture of sorcery. David, as a most unlikely candidate, prevailed with it and ushered his people into a time of great unity and peace.

The mark of the "something more" is neither position nor throwing large amounts of funding at the problem. The something more is a factor of leadership; an influence that brings change from within. Despite Joseph and Daniel being slaves, they never gave in to a slave's heart. As wise stewards of their mantle they faithfully served, and brought God into the equation as they were blessed to be a blessing and in the process wielded change that released God's purposes.

The "something more" is at the heart of biblical leadership.

A Most Unlikely People

The "something more" required to make a difference begins with discerning the strategy God gave the Jewish people, which has enabled them to not only retain their identity, but with disproportionate achievement to serve as catalysts and influencers to the civilizations that would rise and fall around them; like the Greeks, the Romans, the Assyrians, the Ottomans and on and on.

We live in a world seduced. It is a world in which the perception is deemed the reality; where black is seen as white and evil is considered good. The Bible refers to this as the "bondage of corruption." Yet, from the beginning God has had an answer through those known by His Name who, through Him, have been, are and will be a light to the world.

Over the ages, the Jewish people have fulfilled the words of Moses that they would be the head and not the tail. Today with only one-fourth of one percent of the world's population, 27% of all Nobel laureates have gone to Jews since 1950. As a people, Jews have been disproportionate achievers and contributors.

Historically, in civilizations without a middle class, the Jewish people have served that function, as merchants and bankers and people of business. They have been advisors to kings, rulers and leaders and financed national agendas in the societies in which they lived.

Yet, as a people, the Jewish people have been distinctive. As a people, they have released nuggets of wisdom from God's Word that have become the foundations; economically, governmentally, judicially, and morally for what we now call Western civilization. Jewish strategies have resulted in them outliving, as a people, the civilizations of which they have been a part.

A Most Unlikely Strategy

The something more involves a leadership strategy that defies the wisdom of the world; indeed, the wisdom of the ages. Driven by the spiritual, it joins together community to operate as one with the economic. It is a strategy that merges an identity, a spiritual maturity driven by trust and discipline, along with a unique power to form a leadership; all of which is demonstrated "as a people." It is a strategy of righteous power in a corrupt world.

Righteous power builds and brings increase; it wields influence, and is a catalyst for opportunity that brings blessing to those in its sphere.

This leadership strategy begins with a grasp of God's purpose for His own (Genesis 1): to exercise dominion and subdue the earth. Then with an identity and faith in God, as demonstrated by Noah, Abraham, Jacob, Joseph, Moses, David and many other heroes of faith, the mantle is gleaned from Abraham, to be blessed to be a blessing. The model also is from Abraham: of the God-centered, entrepreneurial community.

Within the community of God's people will operate the progressive stewardship of the gifts of its members. Proverbs 31 describes this community-focused entrepreneurial dynamic. The process was outlined by Moses: with a focus on order, ownership and increase.

Deuteronomy 17 outlines the discipline required for leaders: which carries an emphasis of embracing and constantly living according to the principles of God's Word. Then from Moses' father-in-law Jethro, are the steps within the community to nurture and develop leaders. These combined dynamics represent the foundation of Jewish roots and culture from which the strategy of biblical leadership is derived.

Foundations of Jewish Culture

These foundations begin by depending on God and responding to Him with an excellence in employing the model and the mantle. It operates with an identity of being a culture within a culture. It is a nurtured community that expands and builds itself up through trust and tz'dakah.

Its nature is entrepreneurial with a combined thrust of work, service and faith. Its government is self-regulated and originally designed to be self-sustaining. Increase results from the stewardship and service derived from the confluence of the combined gifts of its members.

It exerts leadership on the surrounding community through God-centered wisdom, service and influence. Its advantage is the spiritual authority to employ righteous power within the world's structure, with an impact that like Daniel, holds the potential of being ten times better than the best the world has.

In short, these foundations of an identity, maturity, power and leadership "as a people" are God-centered. The result actuates the impact outlined by Moses in Deuteronomy 28:15 of being "the head and not the tail."

In addressing the realities and turmoil of the times, the growing disparity between light and darkness point to the need to pulling it together in applying righteous power in a corrupt world.

"In the time of the end, many shall be purified and refined, but the wicked shall do wickedly and none of the wicked shall understand; but the wise shall understand. Those who are wise shall shine like the brightness of the sky, and those who lead many to righteousness, like the stars forever and ever." Daniel 12:3, 10-12

Completing It All

Jesus came to do just that: to bring fulfillment, completion to the foundations found in the Jewish roots of the faith.

"I came not to destroy the law and the prophets, but to fulfill." Matthew 5:17

Punctuating the long-accepted strategy of the Jewish people being a culture within a culture, He noted the importance of our distinctive identity within the world.

"You will be in the world, but not of the world." John 17:15, 16

Jesus likewise warned us of the challenges of being a unique people of God.

"These things have I spoken to you, that in Me you might have peace. In the world you will have tribulation, but take courage, I have overcome the world." John 16:33

He also made it clear that the mantle of Abraham, to be blessed to be a blessing, would require our light to shine clearly in the world, in order to point the way to God.

"Let your light so shine before men, that they may see your good works and glorify your Father in Heaven." Matthew 5:16

As these factors work together, God's people are called to transform peoples and nations by teaching them the principles of righteous power by which we all are to live. These principles are what He referred to as the principles of the Kingdom.

"Go, make disciples of the nations, teaching them to observe all I have shown you." Matthew 28:19, 20

The pathway of the Kingdom is as a paradox to the way the world operates. Its focus on God's power rather than ours underlies the premise that in our weakness His strength is manifested. It incorporates an identity of not being like everyone else.

It is a culture of honor that is derived from humility. Its people share a purpose of making their assets work for them (parable of the talents). It stresses ownership without greed, in which ownership increases by sharing. It demands service by which growth comes by generosity; by giving to others. Ambition and destiny are defined by losing your life to find it (dying to self) and advancement coming by yielding. Leadership is demonstrated by serving. Change is brought about by influence. Finally, but not least, perfect love eliminates fear.

Leadership Pathway

So Jesus came to restore the foundations, as it was in the beginning; with the model operated by Abraham. He came to lay an axe to the root of the alliance between the misguided religious elite and the corrupt rulers of the worldly realm.

Jesus came to impart the foundations for true leadership and the strategy and authority that would destroy the works of the devil and the bondage of corruption; to release God's Kingdom rule.

I once asked the Lord why the places He sent us with our economic community development program were such difficult spiritual environments. His answer was immediate and very clear: because His power is best demonstrated by the opportunity and change created in impossible situations. So, it has been with the examples shared in previous chapters.

Biblical Models of Leadership Strategy

Throughout the history of God's people we have models of the impact made through God's leadership strategy. Abraham demonstrated it to the world around him with the God-centered entrepreneurial community model. Isaac (Genesis 29) was a light to the surrounding societies, when by heeding God's voice, he sowed in famine and against all odds reaped abundantly when no others were achieving growth.

Joseph the Patriarch, with a clear God-centered identity, demonstrated the mantle of being blessed to be a blessing (Genesis 39) and became a catalyst of influence in harnessing the resources necessary to give refuge to God's people and bless the Egyptians in the process. Moses outlined the community response for God's people, as a people in giving strict heed to the voice of the Lord (Exodus 15).

David embraced God's heart as the pathway of his destiny and brought God's people into a time of Kingdom rule. Hezekiah brought restoration, liberty and spiritual authority to God's people against numerically more powerful foes. Daniel reshaped and redirected the spiritual climate of the society of which he was a part. Nehemiah gleaned the favor to gain access to the resources of the worldly realm needed for restoring God's people to their roots.

A Society of Leaders

In short, we are not called to be or to operate like everyone else. We are called to be in the world, but not of the world. We're called to be the head and not the tail and to make a difference and to bring change.

Kingdom leaders replicate themselves and mobilize community. They are paradoxes to the way the world operates and employs power.

God's footprint over the ages has been ordinary people doing extraordinary things through the simple things that confound the wise. From this has come the "something more" dimension; a leadership exhibited by God's most unlikely candidates, employing God's most unlikely strategies that has brought about the most unexpected results when those known by His Name achieve the maturity to operate as a society of leaders.

At the core of this strategy is righteous power; the power to overcome the impossible. Paul gave a glimpse of the outcome of this Jewish leadership strategy as releasing the power that would raise the dead (Romans 11:15). Isaiah similarly described a people (Isaiah 58:10, 12) who would operate with a power to rebuild the ancient walls and be the repairers of the breach; a mantle with the ability to fix virtually anything.

"Teach them the principles and precepts and show them the path in which they must walk; then give them the work they must do. Then select from all the people able men, such as fear God, men of truth, hating covetousness; and make them to be rulers of thousands, of hundreds, of fifties, and of tens." Exodus 18:20-21

EPILOGUE

STRATEGY OF ALLIANCES

In the mid-70s, the Lord spoke a word to me from Jeremiah 51. This word defined my calling as an intercessor, while also proving to be foundational to my Joseph-Daniel calling.

"You are My battle-axe and weapon of war: for with you, I will break nations in pieces; with you, I will destroy kingdoms and strongholds; … and with you, I will break in pieces governors and rulers. And I, the Lord, will repay Babylon and Chaldea." Jeremiah 51:20, 23, 24

As "God's battle-axe and weapon of war," there is more than just a hint of going out and paving new territory. There is and has been a distinct challenge to the traditions and methods that may have had application in their time; but are falling short for the tasks ahead. God's battle-axe and weapon of war has a distinct ring of change, of militant change.

The repeated use of the phrase *"with you"* in this Jeremiah 51 passage suggests that the change and territory to be taken will come as a cooperative effort, but will clearly be God-directed. There also is no question as to the extent of the results: "I will break nations in pieces; I will destroy kingdoms and strongholds; I will break in pieces governors and rulers."

Then there was this segment stating: "And I, the Lord, will repay Babylon and Chaldea."

After all the instances in which the scripture used *"with you,"* this segment does not. But it gives implication that because of the previous aligned activities between the prophet and the Lord; that the Lord Himself was then going to do something very dramatic. It bears on the judgment with which He was going "to repay Babylon and Chaldea." The application of this "repayment" in Jeremiah's word followed God's people being taken into Babylonian captivity.

So as I was again meditating on this personally very pivotal word given me years ago, I began discerning additional insights applicable to those of us called as modern-day Josephs and Daniels.

Unholy Gatekeeper Alliances

What I first began seeing was the alliance operating between Babylon as the gatekeeper to the world's business and political system and Chaldea as the source of sorcery-power that operated behind the scenes to control the business-political infrastructure.

A significant parallel to this Babylonian-Chaldean alliance was operating during the days of Elijah. Elijah was confronting a similar union in his incredible face-off with the 450 prophets of Baal and the 400 prophets of Asherah. These were the members of the religious community serving Israel's King Ahab and his Baal-worshipping wife, Jezebel.

Jezebel, the wife of the king of Israel, brought the worship of Baal from Sidon, where her father Ethbaal was king. Jezebel sought to destroy all God's prophets in Israel. Jezebel installed the prophets of Baal and Asherah as part of the royal household. Talk about the enemy penetrating seats of power!

Babylon and Chaldea; idolatry and sorcery; Jezebel and Ahab: the same forces operating against God's earthly infrastructure in the days of Elijah and Jeremiah spiritually represent the pivotal challenge that we have before us today as modern-day Josephs and Daniels.

Yet, the scripture in Jeremiah 51 says, that "I will repay Babylon and Chaldea, says the Lord." This insight bears uniquely on what can be expected as we stand against the same forces of darkness.

So it was, over 200 years after Elijah confronted the minions and results of the Ahab-Jezebel alliance that the Lord spoke to Jeremiah and said, "Through you, I will break nations in pieces; through you I will destroy kingdoms and strongholds ... and I will repay Babylon and Chaldea."

There should be no question as to the extent that idolatry and sorcery have permeated the seats of power of the infrastructures encasing life as we know it today. There should be no question about the operation of modern-day Ahabs and Jezebels, deep in the heart of not only our political and business systems, but our religious institutions, as well. What needs to be brought into focus is the role of today's Kingdom business-community leaders in reclaiming what the enemy has undermined and stolen.

The Relevance for Kingdom Business-Community Leaders

In Revelations 2:20 it was in the church at Thyatira that the false prophetess undermining the efforts of the saints was labeled as "Jezebel." The relevance to the hour we are entering begins gaining clarity for us, as leaders of the business community, when it is recognized that Thyatira was the center of a number of trade guilds, which used the natural resources of the region to make it a very profitable area.

The New Testament church at Thyatira was established by Paul, the tentmaker-apostle, together with Lydia, a known business person. So, Thyatira was a seat of power that was reclaimed by the alliance between Paul and a key business-community leader. The flip side to this equation is that Thyatira was not the only instance the apostle Paul confronted a seat of power that had manifested as an alliance between sorcery and idolatry.

Ephesus was also a commercial, political and spiritual center of the world of Paul's day. It was Aquila and Pricilla, Jewish business people, who took Paul in. They proved very influential in Paul's work with the Corinthians, Ephesians and other sectors of his outreach to the Gentiles. Also at Ephesus, as the work of the Lord progressed, Demetrius incited a riot directed against Paul because he feared the apostle's preaching would threaten his business of selling silver shrines of Diana, the patron goddess of Ephesus.

Paul used a strategy of targeting and aligning himself with the local business community to pioneer significant segments of the early Church. This strategy provoked various manifestations of the idolatry-sorcery alliance. In like fashion, the Church at Thyatira was praised in John's revelation for its works of charity, service, and faith, but was criticized for allowing the followers of Jezebel to prosper in its midst.

Moves of God and the Spirit of Jezebel

So then, who are the followers of Jezebel? Certainly it's more than a convenient label for those we disagree with. Likewise, once identified, what needs to be done to deny them the opportunity to prosper in our midst?

A clue to their identity, tied back to this word of repaying Babylon and Chaldea, is given in Acts 6 and 7. The context is described in verses 7-10 of Acts 6:

"Then the Word of God spread, and the number of the disciples multiplied greatly in Jerusalem, and a great many of the priests were obedient to the faith. And Stephen, full of faith and power, did great wonders and signs among the people. Then there arose some from what is called the Synagogue of the Freedmen, disputing with Stephen. And they were not able to resist the wisdom and the Spirit by which he spoke."

When the power of God is operating, and the wisdom and the Spirit are flowing, there will be those who resist.

The initial response to Stephen, when those he was interacting with couldn't resist the truth of his words and power of the Spirit was that they used false witnesses, accused Stephen, and stirred up first the people, then the leadership.

Religious spirits resist the power of God and moves of His Spirit. The ugly, religious backlash Stephen experienced reflects the dynamic that has emerged in centuries past and still exists today when the power of God, the truth of God and Spirit of God are in evidence and are bringing change. There will be those who not only resist, but who will do everything within their power to undermine what they fail to recognize as being from God.

Sorcery: Infiltration Alliances and Tactics

The Jezebels are those who undermine the power of God and the moves of the Spirit of the Lord.

As we see the gates opening to a major move of God in the marketplace, we need to be wise and alert. The spirit of Jezebel is not limited by gender. The Jezebels are the major source of division operating against the righteous in gatekeeper functions. The Jezebels operate as sorcerers, with a power derived by age-old Chaldean divination. The Jezebels have been and continue to be found hidden in centers of fervent religious and spiritual activities.

Yet the operation of Jezebels will only be in part, until they become allied with an Ahab.

The Jezebels who envy, hate, divide and seek to destroy those who operate by the Spirit of the Lord, cannot accomplish their surreptitious tasks without seducing or beguiling the gatekeeper. The Ahabs are the gatekeepers into the seats of power within our religious, business and political institutions. They are gatekeepers, who are naively enticed and controlled by the Jezebels and their evil intentions.

So, then after identifying the Jezebels, the issue is to insure they are rendered ineffective and removed from our midst.

Unholy alliances can and will be pulled down by the power, anointing and wisdom of God. But in similar fashion to Jezebel's removal, it is going to take divinely appointed alliances, such as reflected by Jehu and Elisha to accomplish the task.

The Jehu-Elisha alliance came only after Elijah's incredible, supernatural encounter with the prophets of Baal and Asherah. Elijah's role was an essential first step in the dismantling of this Ahab-Jezebel alliance. Elijah's face-off not only removed the infrastructure of the prophets of Baal and Asherah, but it resulted in the hearts of the people being turned back to the Lord. Yet despite his incredible boldness in this divinely appointed engagement; a spiritually exhausted Elijah became overwhelmed at the prospect of encountering Jezebel and fled.

It took Elijah's protégé Elisha and Jehu, a man of authority under Ahab, to finally pull down the heart of this unholy alliance, Jezebel herself. It was the cooperative alliance between Elisha and Jehu that accomplished this task. This alliance gives significant insight into the roles that can be expected from the alliances of today's Josephs and Daniels and their counterparts. These are the alliances that will play into a fulfillment of God's promise to repay Babylon and Chaldea.

Joseph's Brothers and Chaldea

During his eloquent and anointed response to the council of accusers he faced, Stephen spoke about the necessity of God leading Abraham out of Mesopotamia, also known, as the land and sphere of the Chaldeans. THIS was a requirement and necessity for Abraham to be positioned to receive God's promise.

Stephen also spoke of the envy the brothers of Joseph had for him. The envy operating among Joseph's brothers and the dishonor they sowed within the land of Promise were undermining the purposes God promised to their forefather Abraham. Something had to change.

In addressing the realities of that change, God had a crucible designed to prepare Joseph for the authority required for him to effectively overcome the Jezebels of Egypt and the power associated with the envy of his brothers.

According to Psalm 105:17, the Lord sent Joseph before them to prepare the way for God's purposes for His people. Joseph was the forerunner God used, not only to circumvent the coming disruptions, but to bring about the change needed to position God's people to inherit His covenant promises.

Yet over the centuries, the struggle has again and again been centered on God's people being enticed and beguiled by the flavor of Chaldea; of finding it easier to believe the supernatural that comes from the evil one than to believe in the God of miracles. The flavor of Chaldea was represented by prophets of Baal and Asherah and was established by unholy alliances. Its impact was cycles of unbelief and disobedience resulting in bondage for God's people.

However, the scripture in Jeremiah says that: *"I will repay Babylon and Chaldea, says the Lord."*

The Alliance of the Ages

Chaldea and Babylon; Jezebel and Ahab; witchcraft and mammon; sorcery and idolatry are each simply different dimensions of the same alliance: the unholy alliance of the ages.

Babylon and Chaldea clearly represent the alliance of the gate-keepers of the world's commercial and political infrastructure with sorcery, the occult. However, the world's system as a whole is only a means to an end. That end is the employment of power through the unholy alliances of idolatry and sorcery; witchcraft and mammon.

The challenge is in bringing change, which begins with assuming responsibility. That will involve entering the gates and challenging these occult seats of power; to bring disruption that releases a shift of power. This spiritual shift of power was evidenced in the Apostle Paul's exploits as he pioneered his way into the bastions of the evil one in the first century.

This is our Father's world. The earth is the Lord's and the fullness thereof. What is commonly labeled as the world's system reflects a misappropriation of God's creation and the resources reflected by the Psalmist's insight that the Lord owns the cattle on a thousand hills.

The accomplishment of God initiatives for these days advance repossessing what rightfully belongs to the Lord. THAT will often involve instances of God-ordained alliances with gatekeepers of the world's infrastructures, like Pharaoh and Cyrus, as the Lord sovereignly restores what belongs to Him in the accomplishment of His end-time purposes.

Turbulence may surround these agendas. Disruptions may hit economies of the world. The time of His power will indeed be accompanied by a time of His judgment. But the disruptions will provide opportunity for those with unusual calls of God, to be used uniquely for the Lord's redemptive purposes within the midst of these domains referred to as the world's system.

Over the centuries, the Lord has used counter-alliance emissaries to intervene in the affairs of men to strategically circumvent the countdown resulting from these evil alliances. There are ample examples in Scripture of heroes of faith, who break in pieces and destroy the foundations of these age-old, evil alliances. Examples like Joseph and Daniel and Ezra and Nehemiah, who by the Spirit of the Lord and the authority entrusted to them, reversed the power of unholy alliances and implanted righteous power. God's ambassadors and emissaries, leaders in the business and political arena, have been and will be called to work along side secular gatekeepers in seats of power in the accomplishment of God's purposes.

These age-old alliances between witchcraft and mammon; between sorcery and idolatry serve to entice and divide God's people and undermine God's purposes. Yet, "I will repay Babylon and Chaldea, says the Lord." So the Lord will again intervene to bring judgment on those who entice his people into unbelief and idolatry; and those who seek to undermine and stymie His purposes. Extraordinary God-initiatives and changes can be expected within the world's infrastructure where the occult has become the resident seat of power.

Likewise, God's modern-day agendas to repay Babylon and Chaldea will also manifest where religious traditions of men align with the spirit of Chaldea and Babylon to rage against the initiatives released by the Spirit of God.

However, this judgment of repayment will be released only after the thrust of what Jeremiah saw as the cooperative efforts described by: "With you, I will break nations in pieces; with you I will destroy kingdoms and strongholds."

The Role of the Josephs and Daniels

Modern-day Josephs and Daniels; and this entire move of God into the marketplace reflects God's throne-room strategy designed to penetrate the world's commercial and political infrastructures. The Josephs and Daniels cross boundaries that the traditional Church just doesn't tend to venture into. The Josephs and Daniels are catalysts releasing the process of restoring God's covenant principles and rule. Their role is in restoring and operating with a Kingdom perspective within the fabric of society.

Today's Josephs and Daniels understand God's concept of community: how business and community are designed to operate together as it was revealed to the patriarchs and outlined in Deuteronomy. The Josephs and Daniels understand the admonitions in Isaiah 58 to reach out to the hungry and the oppressed as a significant part of being community-builders. It's where the Gospel of salvation and the social Gospel collide and become the Gospel of the Kingdom.

Today's Josephs and Daniels will encounter confrontations with these age-old alliances. Yet, like Daniel, those who truly operate through God will be strong and will do exploits. They will operate in the authority and anointing that was evidenced when Joseph was elevated to sit along side of Pharaoh. The confrontations will be about the restoration of God's Kingdom rule. The Josephs and Daniels will penetrate the heart of darkness and the seats of power that control what was originally designed to be a part of God's Kingdom. The Josephs and Daniels will work along side the Pharaohs and Cyruses of our day to restore what God has all along meant for His own.

Additionally, this move of God in the marketplace will not only serve to create holy alliances between modern-day Josephs and Daniels and their gatekeeper counterparts, but it will see a mobilization within the business community that will result in:

- releasing the believing business community into the walk of God's Kingdom;
- of releasing the anointing into their respective businesses to assume responsibility for their communities and resources, and of
- redeeming the believing community's businesses, business people and finances for the Lord.

God's anointed business community bears a unique calling. It includes spiritually liberating the common man by eliminating the gap between the sacred and the secular. Those so aligning themselves with God will see the walls coming down between business and ministry.

The role of God's business community includes restoring the kingly, leadership function of God's people through a strategy of holy alliances that counter and defeat the prevailing unholy alliances.

Historically, the Jewish people have developed community to an advanced, mature stature. It is community that eschews elitism and nurtures opportunity as it draws its members as a whole together. The Rothschilds created alliances sought out by the world and progressively and proactively enhanced the standing of Jews as a people. Community without cultivating-alliances falls far short of the Body maturity written of by Paul in Ephesians 4.

The Strategy of Alliances

Ariel Sharon's autobiography "Warrior" illustrates how an alliance was mobilized to break the stranglehold of oppression that had crept into the seats of power; in this case, within Israel at the time.

The 20th chapter of Mr. Sharon's book describes the need for the formation of the Likud party in Israel. The evolution of power within the Labor party had sadly digressed from the significant role its leaders had played in Israel's war for independence. What had resulted in just three decades in Israel was the exclusion of anyone outside Labor's members and support system from receiving the benefits that should have been afforded to all the citizenry. There was simply a bureaucratic stranglehold on jobs, housing, bank loans, education, social services and so forth. An unholy alliance, if you will, operated through the bureaucratic infrastructure.

The Likud party became an alliance of necessity for all those outside the Labor infrastructure. It included a host of diverse groups who previously may have been at odds with one another. These were groups who otherwise might not have taken the time to sit down at the same table. Yet the reality of the situation had a very real need for the power of unity that could only come from a "counter" alliance: a counter alliance to challenge the status quo.

The believing business community today holds a similar potential. It is the potential of overthrowing the bastions of unholy gatekeepers and penetrating key seats of power operating within the world's business and political systems. Those called in this way, understand.

Anointed business leaders operate across boundaries that those in traditional ministerial circles too often would not consider breaching. Those genuinely called as Josephs and Daniels comprise a balance of administrative gifts of getting things done; with leadership skills that are not constrained by Pharisaical exclusivity and tradition; with a sensitivity and commitment to hearing God's voice with a focus on the priorities of His heart. It begins with assuming the responsibility and cost of the mantle.

God's move into the marketplace is the move of God for this hour. It is a move of God exceeding in significance and impact, the rise of the parachurch movement of the late 50's.

We are entering the time in which the Lord will repay Babylon and Chaldea. Alliances will be key in setting the stage for this throne-room strategy. These are holy alliances that unseat the Jezebel's and restore God's kingdom rule. These are alliances that operate in simplicity, yet potency to challenge the status quo and barriers to God's redemptive purposes for this hour.

An important aspect of this dynamic was recognized in an article carried in the Wall Street Journal ("Independent's Day," August 28, 2002) about how several smaller ad agencies teamed up to compete for the very large Chrysler account. The observation of the article was that independent business alliances are hot because they capture the creativity of the independent entrepreneurs, something that was seen missing in the stifling bureaucracy of the larger agencies.

The vice-like grip and pervasive nature of today's unholy alliances of idolatry and sorcery are necessitating unusual action from God's people. This is action reflecting an understanding of the times, with a knowledge of what to do. It is action that will require diverse groups aligning themselves and creating holy alliances to accomplish God's purposes for this hour. It is action not constrained by political correctness, denominational purity or a watered-down Gospel.

Unusual alliances will therefore result. These will be alliances that begin at the level reflecting Jesus' wisdom of sending His people into enemy territory, two by two. They will incorporate cooperative efforts between existing networks and coalitions. They will reflect alliances between businesses and ministries; alliances between modern-day Josephs and Pharaohs.

Alliances among God's entrepreneurs will serve to harness the power of unity to push back the encroachment of darkness into arenas God intended for good. Over the ages, community entrepreneurs have been those called as pioneers to pave the way for God's agendas. Community entrepreneurs today are modeled after the patriarchs, with their modus operandi outlined in the God-centered, entrepreneurial community principles found in Scripture and out-lined in this book.

The need calls for not only just alliances within the business community; but alliances between the business community and those uniquely called intercessors, who have been anointed to understand the times. These will be alliances that pull down the bar-riers between business and ministry. They will be alliances at the community level, as well as alliances that penetrate seats of power at the national level. These will be holy alliances that connect God's marketplace ambassadors for this hour, across the globe.

Judgment is clearly coming to Babylon and Chaldea. The pro-cess is underway as the Lord positions those with unique callings to serve together with Him in breaking nations in pieces, of destroying kingdoms and strongholds. The penetration of the world's system by God's modern-day marketplace emissaries is going to unfold with simplicity. It will be a simplicity marked with a sovereign coordination of strategically called individuals and groups. These are individuals and groups — entrepreneurs and business leaders — who form alliances which will break the stranglehold represented by Jezebel and Ahab, by witchcraft and mammon, by sorcery and idolatry. These are individuals, groups and alliances who as it was said of Daniel, are those who know their God and will do exploits.

APPENDIX

PRAYER FOR HEARING GOD MORE CLEARLY

Lord God, in the Name of Jesus, I come boldly before your throne. Cleanse my heart O God. Thank You that I am cleansed by the blood of Jesus and I have invited the Holy Spirit to live within me. I bring every thought of my mind and every impression in my heart into captivity to the obedience of Jesus. Lord, I want to hear what You have to say. I trust You to communicate to me.

And in the Name of Jesus, I take authority over every soulish stronghold along with every demonic and interfering spirit. I forbid any enemy activity to operate in my mind or soul. I open my heart to the Holy Spirit—to inspire, to guide, to illuminate and reveal to me truth, insights and perspectives that will anoint my efforts in planning for my business.

I take authority over fear, anxiety, doubt and unbelief in the name of Jesus. I bind any negative, critical or condemning spirits in the Name of Jesus and forbid you to interfere with or in any way to imitate God's voice to me.

Lord, I thank you for being in charge of every aspect of my being and for all that will unfold in this process. I look forward to growing in this new dimension with you and for what You have planned for me through it. In the Name of Jesus. Amen.

APPENDIX

WEEKLY FINANCIAL REPORT

WEEKLY FINANCIAL REPORT

CASH-CLOSE LAST WEEK $_____
DEPOSITS THIS WEEK $_____
CASH CLOSE THIS WEEK $_____

ACCOUNTS RECEIVABLE (MONIES OWED TO YOU)
  CLOSE **LAST WEEK** $_____
COLLECTED THIS WEEK $_____
BILLED THIS WEEK $_____
ACCOUNTS RECEIVABLE
  CLOSE **THIS WEEK** $_____

ACCOUNTS PAYABLE (MONIES YOU OWE)
  CLOSE **LAST WEEK** $_____
ACCOUNTS PAYABLE
  PAID THIS WEEK $_____
NEW BILLS THIS WEEK $_____
ACCOUNTS PAYABLE
  CLOSE **THIS WEEK** $_____

MONTHLY SALES
    CLOSE LAST WEEK $_____

SALES THIS WEEK $_____

MONTHLY SALES
    CLOSE THIS WEEK $_____

APPENDIX

ELEMENTS OF THE BUSINESS PLAN

- **Market Need and Background**

- **Your Company and the Key Player(s)**

- **Your Product/Service**

- **Benefits (to customers)**

- **The Customer**

- **Annual Sales and Budget**

- **Initial Funding (equipment, advertising)**

- **Goals and Strategies**

- **The Opportunity (describe)**

- **Your Vision as a Community Builder**

APPENDIX

PLANNING ELEMENTS TO MENTOR COMMUNITY BUILDERS

- **The Natural Gifts**

- **The Spiritual Gifts**

- **The Dream ...in Serving Others**

- **The Gateways of Opportunity**

- **The Vision as a Community Builder**

- **Those Being Served**

- **The Mentors**

- **The Goals for Five Years from Now**

- **Strategies for the Community Good**

APPENDIX

SPIRITUAL GIFT DESCRIPTIONS

Servers will take on tasks wholehearted and stick to it until it is done, even if it means personal sacrifice. They tend be aware of others' preferences and remember details well. They prefer projects where they can see immediate results. Reassurance and recognition are important motivators for servers. They are doers, self-starters, dependable and can work alone very well. Martha in the Gospels was a server.

Prophetic gifted believers operate with a balance between hearing from God and a sense of righteousness. They embrace biblical truths and proactively seek to discern what the Holy Spirit is saying. When they KNOW they have heard from God, they will act; and need to discern between first stages of hearing and the "full counsel" needed to act upon. When this gift is mature, there will be a confidence that knows when to speak the Word of the Lord versus when to pray. Words given by prophetic people carry authority and result.

Givers are ones who sense God's heart where needs are concerned. Combined with their other gifts, Givers break the mold of the status quo. They tend toward being creative or leaders and sometimes both; which ties into their response to fixing situations that are due to the lack of resource. Givers can be very effective entrepreneurs. In many instances, they will take great joy in giving without the need for credit. Yet in others, simple appreciation is important to them.

Teachers enjoy connecting the dots and studying God's Word. They encourage others to embrace biblical truths. Teachers tend to use Biblical examples more than personal examples when punctuating truth. Teachers are intellectually inclined and sticklers for detail. They tend to relate to others in light of how closely their lives adhere to God's Word.

Exhorters exercise a gift that is "life-related." They draw upon life experiences in order to encourage and enhance a God-centered purposefulness and fruitfulness in others. They typically are loving and well-liked, exhibiting positive attitudes toward nurturing maturity and growth in others. They are able to see the "steps" others need to reach their goals or to extract themselves from trials.

Mercy-gifted people are ones who are motivated to help others when they recognize a particular need. They are strong in extending encouragement to those undergoing distress. They extend hope to the wavering and hopeless; and expect the seeds they plant will bear fruit. They tend to be sensitive to protecting others against words and actions that may hurt others. They often operate with a strong discernment of what is happening behind the superficial.

Leaders have a natural ability to lead and direct others. They are people of action who love to "make things happen." They facilitate agendas and tasks for others. They don't hesitate in drawing and acting on conclusions. They tend to be big-picture people, who are able to view things from a long-term perspective. They typically are planners and organizers. Once goals are established they enjoy the process of implementing the steps toward goals.

The Entrepreneurial gift is not one of the specific Romans 12 motivational gifts. However, God's nature is to create, innovate, build and multiply. When those dimensions of God's DNA operate within a person, they manifest as an entrepreneurial gift. When the entrepreneurial is particularly strong, it bleeds into and complements ones other strengths, that being their specific motivational gifts. Those strong in this dynamic will typically do well with starting and succeeding in those own business. Those with entrepreneurial scores less than 40 may prove to need partner(s) in the start/operation of their own business.

AUTHOR

Morris E. Ruddick

Entrepreneur, consultant, minister and business owner, Morris Ruddick has led development of entrepreneurial activities in critical needy areas and brought together combined business-ministry initiatives in several nations, with a focus on assisting believers in lands of persecution and distress. Mr. Ruddick's Kingdom agendas reflect a unique merging of the secular and the spiritual with initiatives based on biblical principles of business. Since 1995, he has been at the forefront of encouraging and mobilizing spiritually-minded business leaders to step out in faith by combining their entrepreneurial and spiritual gifts to build communities and impact their nations.

In the last few years Mr. Ruddick's Kingdom agendas have spanned five continents with hands-on activities in Russia, Belarus, Nigeria, Ethiopia, Botswana, South Africa, Italy, India, Afghanistan, China, Vietnam and Israel. His Kingdom business initiatives have included entrepreneurial startup programs, training for spiritual business leaders and community building strategies for lands of persecution and oppression. His programs are based on the biblical model of sowing and reaping in famine. He helped organize and launch, and continues serving as board member for the Joseph Project, an Israeli-based international consortium of humanitarian aid that assists Israeli immigrants and citizens.

Israel's Technology Incubator Program is listed among the clients he has served. He is a former board member of the Nehemiah

Fund, an Israeli non-profit (amuta) that has provided grants to members of Israel's believing community facing economic distress.

Mr. Ruddick is as an elder and board-member of the one-newman congregation of Church in the City-Beth Abraham. He spent 19 years on the board of Marilyn Hickey Ministries and Orchard Road Christian Center where he was Chairman of both the Compensation and Audit Committees. He is a member of the Messianic Jewish Alliance. He served as Corporate Secretary of the International Christian Chamber of Commerce-USA and is a board member of Love Botswana Outreach. His activities also include being board advisor to the Kingdom Chamber of Commerce for Africa, as well as the Creation Institute. He has been a national speaker and workshop leader for the National Religious Broadcasters, Mike and Cindy Jacob's Out of the Box Marketplace Conferences, the GCOWE Missions Conference, Os Hillman's Marketplace Ministry Leader's Summit, Peter Wagner's Roundtable on Kingdom Wealth, the Kingdom Economic Yearly Summit (KEYS); and as a part of the editorial advisory board of the *Journal of Ministry Marketing and Management*.

Over the years, he has served executive suite management with his planning and strategy development talents in a diversity of progressive mid-sized operations, ministry groups, and Fortune 500 companies. He has been at the helm of designing and implementing two successful corporate turnarounds, one being for a $1.4 billion firm.

His time as a US Marine Corps officer during the height of the Vietnam conflict included leading both infantry and recon units, as well as serving as a senior battalion advisor with the Vietnamese Marine Corps. He headed up the mobile training team program that prepared parachute-scuba qualified Marines (Force Recon) for reconnaissance and special operations. Mr. Ruddick was awarded the Silver Star, two Bronze Stars, the Navy Commendation Medal and the Vietnamese Medal of Honor for his actions in combat.

He holds ordination papers from the United Christian Ministerial Association, a BS from Northwestern University; and an MS in communications and doctoral work in statistics; as well as a year of biblical studies at Oral Roberts University.

CONTACT INFORMATION

To contact the author
to speak at your conference or gathering of marketplace leaders,
please write

Morris Ruddick
Global Initiatives Foundation
P.O. Box 370291
Denver, CO 80237 USA

or email:

info@strategic-initiatives.org

or call 303.741-9000 and leave a message

You may wish to visit the Global Initiatives Foundation website. It
contains additional information.
The website address is:

http://www.strategic-initiatives.org

The Strategic Intercession Global Network (SIGN) contains additional articles:

www.strategicintercession.org

CPSIA information can be obtained at www.ICGtesting.com
Printed in the USA
BVOW030503241012

303770BV00003B/2/P

9 781624 195662